Compact City

THE NEXT URBAN EVOLUTION

IN RESPONSE TO CLIMATE CHANGE

Thomas Saaty

saaty@katz.pitt.edu

Compact City
The Next Urban Evolution
in Response to Climate Change

Thomas L. Saaty
saaty@katz.pitt.edu

Library of Congress Catalog Card Number: to be obtained when text is complete

Copyright 2013 by RWS Publications, Pittsburgh, PA

ISBN 10 digit: 1-888603-12-7
ISBN 13 digit: 978-1-888603-12-5

Printed in the United States of America

To the memory of my friend and co-author of the first edition of this book, George Bernard Dantzig (1914-2005), the inventor of the Simplex Process in Linear Programming

TABLE OF CONTENTS

Preface

This book is about cities of the future. It is a follow up and an updating of a book called Compact City that I coauthored with George Dantzig in 1973, and later translated to Japanese and Russian. We need to control nature by eliminating its capricious threats to our lives. We do it best by not only making our living, working , sports and other leisure structures more accessible in space, but also by minimizing and banishing congestions and the need for long times to commute to work or to access shopping malls, sports and cultural activities. With the threat of global warming and melting of the polar ice cap in the Antarctic, low lying cities throughout the world are threatened with drowning under more than 150 feet of water. What should we be thinking about insulating ourselves from natural threats like hurricanes and tsunamis and earthquakes? Surprisingly enough, the new design will eliminate one of the problems of poverty, the lack of shelter.

My thanks for help in producing this book go to my dedicated and tireless colleague Professor William Hefley; to my former student and frequent coauthor in decision theory the brilliant Dr. Kirti Peniwati from Jakarta, Indonesia; to the honors student, Gavin White at my university, who helped by writing the summary Chapter 4 of the original Compact City; to my friend from Chengdu, China, Dr. Daji Ergu for helping me identify and include pictures of malls from the Internet; to Christina Graziano for reading and commenting on parts of the manuscript; to Professor Mujgan Sagir at Osmangazi University in Eskisehir, Turkey, for coauthoring a paper with me on city rankings using my Analytic Hierarchy Process theory, published in JSSE at Tsinghua

University (often called China's MIT) in Beijing, China; to my five students from the Indian Institute of Management at Indore for their example in Chapter 6: Vikas Soni, Sunil Prabhu, KrishanTyagi', Gaurav Singhal, and Rejath Nair; to my niece Leila Barclay and her daughter Nadia for reading, making changes and adding material to the manuscript; my thanks also go to Professor Patrick Harker for editing Chapters 5 and 6 and to his wife (my daughter) Emily for editing Chapter 3; for their twins Meghan Chapter 1 and Michael Chapter 2 and my son Daniel Chapter 4; to IBM for financial support to develop and produce this work, and to my beloved wife Rozann who worked tirelessly to perfect the manuscript.

Chapter 1

The Evolution of Cities

INTRODUCTION

It is likely that if, instead of Manhattan allowing skyscrapers to sprout at random, it was built as a holistic integrated 3-dimensional compact city, the perfect storm of 2012, Hurricane Sandy, would have had no effect on its internal activities and little on its external activities. We need to organize the continuity of our living and avoid nature's control over us. That is certain to be our future.

From the time that we are children, born in a certain place, we take our environment for granted. We think and behave as if it is ordained to be that way and thus tend to resist change. Look at how people, who live in a hurricane-prone region and have experienced much destruction and loss, continue to live in that region even after several repetitions. They do not seek safer areas for permanent relocation, often staying and suffering the consequences of an oncoming disaster and not even moving to safer areas temporarily. Perhaps this is because the unknown is threatening.

Deciding on where and how to live primarily depends on one's conditioning and circumstances. If one lives in open spaces, one would tend to prefer open spaces and find it hard and strange to live in close quarters, unless of course one is accorded privileges that appeal to one's values and that can compensate for the differences, as those know today who live in cities like Paris and New York. A person living early in the eighteen hundreds would never have been supportive of building a three dimensional Manhattan as it is today. The third dimension would have seemed threatening in size as it inhibits getting to open spaces.

This manuscript makes three contributions. First, it informs and alerts the reader about the urgent need to get involved in the process of designing and building new cities of the future. Second, it advocates experimentation with building three dimensional compact cities along the lines originally proposed by Dantzig and Saaty in their innovative book Compact City. There are many reasons why this may be required to minimize or eliminate traffic problems and congestions that challenge people's patience and health, conserve energy, speed up social integration, mitigate possible environmental disasters, and preserve civilization and progress as we know them today.

The third contribution is how to make decisions and choices scientifically and comprehensively using the judgments of experts as to what, how, and where to expand or locate cities of the future. In particular compact cities may need higher altitudes to avoid the dangers of the melting five million square mile area that is two miles high that is the South Pole ice cap, whose melting would cause the sea level to rise by more than 140 feet inundating many low lying areas such as coastal cities and islands throughout the world, but they still need proximity to water and other natural resources for growing food. To see this dramatic rise, we know that the earth as a perfect sphere is 200,000,000 sq. mi. in area and the two-mile-high five-million-square-mile ice cap of Antarctica can be sliced horizontally into two times 5,280 or a total of about 10,500 slabs of one-foot-thick ice and five million square mile area. Forty such slabs cover the earth once to a depth of one foot, and thus the total will cover it to a depth of 252 feet. This inundation could be the result of global warming.

THE WORLD WITH MORE THAN 7 BILLION IN POPULATION

It was announced on 31 October 2011 that the world population had reached 7 billion. In 1998, when the world population was 5.9 billion, the United Nations predicted that by 2050 the world population would be 8.9 billion, only to revise it two years later, upward to 9.3 billion, indicating a turn in the birth rate. Rising U.S. and European birthrates were among the factors causing the revised prediction. The Population Reference Bureau reported in its 2012 World population data sheet that now the world population is almost 7.1 billion, with developing countries accounting for 97% of this growth.

Population projections are sensitive to changes in assumptions about future fertility rates. There have been different plausible scenarios: for the next 40 years the world population might either end up at only eight billion or grow to 10.5 billion. A more recent UN projection was based on assuming a decline in the global fertility rate to 2.02 by 2050, and eventually to 1.85, with the total world population gradually decreasing by the end of this century. Other sources of the uncertainty are the possible relaxation of China's one-child policy, fewer funds for foreign aids, and social/cultural resistance to birth control. Despite the many uncertainties, governments, international agencies, and private corporations depend on demographic projections for making decisions in planning their strategy and long-term investments.

DISTRIBUTION OF THE POPULATION

The growth of cities is not a new phenomenon. For example, the village of Rome was probably founded sometime in the 8th century BC. Rome grew into an imperial city, the largest urban center of its time in the world, with a population of about one million inhabitants. Even then Rome experienced ancient versions of the same modern day problems facing many cities today. This included traffic congestions so severe that Julius Caesar once proposed a ban on chariot traffic during the day because of the crowding and the din of hooves and clatter of iron chariot wheels.

A document issued by the Population Division of the United Nations reported that in mid-2009 the world urban population crossed the 50% mark. Over 53% of the world's total urban population of 3.5 billion lives in towns with less than 500,000 people. About 1.16 billion of them or one third live in towns with less than 100,000 people. Only about 9% of the world's urban population lives in the existing 27 mega-cities of more than 10 million people.

There is a wide variety of city sizes in the world. The Appendix at the end of this book lists all the cities with a million or more population. By 2030, the population living in larger cities is expected to reach almost 5 billion and many will be poor. Incidentally, all people will have a roof over their heads were the plan of this book to be followed. In Europe, 67% of urban dwellers live in cities with fewer than half a million people and only 10 percent live in cities with 5 million people or more. In Asia, Latin

America, the Caribbean and North America, about one in every five urban dwellers lives in a large urban agglomeration. Only 37% live in large cities. The proportion of urban dwellers living in small cities is about 50% in Asia, Latin America and the Caribbean. In North American only 37% live in small cities.

In Africa 58% of urban dwellers live in smaller cities with less than 500 thousand inhabitants and only 9% live in cities with more than 5 million inhabitants.

Urban populations have a fast growth. The world's urban population grew very rapidly over the 20th century, by more than 10 times, from 220 million to 2.8 billion. While 15% of the world population lived in cities early in the twentieth century, the percentage grew to more than 50 percent (3.3 billion) by 2008. Five billion people are expected to live in larger cities by 2030. However, during the next few decades, the developing world will see even faster growth than in the 20th century, especially in Africa and Asia where the urban population has been projected to double between 2000 and 2030 (in a single generation), when 81% of the world's urban population will live in what is today the developing world.

Today Asia has half the world's urban population and Africa's urban population is more than that of North America. Europe, which had more than half of the world's 100 largest cities early in the 20th century had only 10 of them in 2000, and had none of the world's 100 fastest-growing cities in terms of population growth rates between 1950 and 2000. Rather it has most of the world's slowest growing (and declining) cities. A majority of Europe's great centers of industry are no longer among the world's largest cities.

Data from the Census Bureau of the U.S. reveals that currently 79 percent of Americans live in urban areas. Only slightly more than 5 percent lived in urban areas in the 1790's; the number had tripled by 1850, and surpassed 50 percent by 1920.

A German government study done late in 2009 indicated that their population approximately 82 million population will decrease by 12 to 17 million people while experiencing a significant shift in its demographic profile. The most significant finding from this study is the projected shift in the share of senior citizens and children. Together they are expected to increase from 40% to 50% of the entire country's population. The expected ratio of senior citizens to children will be 2:1 by 2040, because of the trend towards an ageing population. A renewed focus on planning for future investments has been initiated with an eye on effective and efficient resource allocation of social services.

THE BEGINNING OF CIVILIZATION

Sumer, the "land of the civilized lords", is the homeland of the world's earliest civilization. It occupied roughly the same territory between the Tigris and Euphrates as the part of Iraq from near Baghdad to the Persian Gulf. The land was identified with the Biblical Garden of Eden because of its productivity. It was first settled in about 4500 BC by the Ubaidians, who founded villages which later became important Sumerian urban centers. Around 4000 BCE the Sumerians moved into Mesopotamia, most likely from around the Caspian Sea. By 3800 BCE the Sumerians had supplanted the Ubaidians and Semites in southern Mesopotamia.

They had built better canals for irrigating and transporting crops. Around 3500 BC, the time of its greatest success and prosperity, Sumeria consisted of more than a dozen walled city-states, the most widely known were Eridu, Kish, Lagash, Uruk, Ur, and Nippur. Large cities grew to a population of 20,000 to 40,000 people. The city of Uruk (the origin of the name Iraq) probably had a population of around 45,000 at the end of Sumerian era. Each city was surrounded by many villages and hamlets. Their streets were narrow and winding. The outstanding feature of each city was the temple built on a tower, situated on a high terrace known as a ziggurat, which had ramps or staircases winding up around the exterior. Besides planting and harvesting crops, the Sumerians hunted, fished, and raised domestic animals.

The land where Sumerians had settled was mostly swamp. It was a river delta that could only be made habitable by large-scale irrigation and flood control. The Sumerians developed an excellent irrigation system that made it possible to grow a substantial agricultural industry, so that for the first time in human history, wheat farming and raising cattle were performed on a large scale. The Sumerians brought to early human civilization numerous technological inventions: about 3500 BC, the wheel made of a solid piece of wood was used in ass-drawn war chariots, the potter's wheel replaced molding clay by hand and was the first human mechanical device , melting copper with zinc produced the harder than copper bronze metal, the plough, daggers, burnt bricks, the architectural arch, leather, chisels, hammers, braces, bits, nails, pins, needles, rings, hoes, axes, knives, arrowheads, swords, glue, water skins, lance points, bags, harnesses, armor, quivers, scabbards, boots, sandals, harpoons, and beer brewing.

Sumer, called Shumer by their Akkadian neighbors, dominated the ancient world, spiritually and culturally, for more than a millennium. The stories of the great flood as told in the Bible and in the Sumerian legend of Gilgamesh, have too many nearly identical passages to be coincidental. Observant, reflective, and pragmatic, the Sumerians evolved a way of life that struck a balance between reason and fancy, freedom and authority. As a consequence, they made outstanding technological and ideological breakthroughs. A friend, Igor Ushakov, in his book *Histories of Scientific Insights, 2007,* wrote about human insights and creativity that the Sumerian inventions and innovations easily place them among the most creative cultures in human pre-history and history. It is possible that the descendants of the people of Ur who were Sumerians (the ancestors of the Jewish people of today – there is a Jewish US Senator from New York whose family name is Schumer) were also creative in the way they envisioned their God in the biblical book of Genesis. There is the story of God and His entourage dropping in for lunch prepared by Sarai, Abram's wife (changed by God to Abraham at age 99 and Sarai to Sarah).

CHINA'S POPULATION WITH INCREASING HIGHER INCOME CLASSES

China's local and national leaders face a huge challenge in coping with the country's expansion of cities. The McKinsey Global Institution (MGI), projects that China's urban population would expand from 572 million in 2005 to 926 million in 2025, and would reach 1 billion by 2030. This means that 350 million people will be added to China's urban population by 2025, more than the population of the United States today. China's cities have been expanding over the past two decades and will continue to expand over the next 20 years. There will ultimately be 221 cities in China, each with more than 1 million people.

Over the past 15 years, megacities with more than 10 million people have emerged in China. Over the next 20 years it is predicted that there will be six more, of which two would have more than 20 million people. The McKinsey Global Institution estimates that 41 percent of China's higher income classes, compared with 11 percent in 2005, will live in them. The trend points to China heading toward a dispersed urbanization pattern with more noticeable expansion in the number of midsized and small cities.

China's pattern of urbanization will be different in the future from what it has been in the last 15 years. Migration is expected to drive urbanization at a higher rate. Between 1990 and 2005, MGI estimates that 103 million people migrated from rural to urban areas, accounting for 32 percent of the urban population increase. MGI projects that by 2025 about 64 percent of the Chinese population will live in cities. By then 243 million new migrants, in addition to the 103 million mentioned above, will represent almost 40 percent of the total urban population. Migration will have driven almost 70 percent of the urban population growth from 2005 to 2025.

The McKinsey Global Institution grouped the urbanization pressures into the following four main categories.

1) *Land and* spatial development: There will be intense tension between the loss of arable land on one hand, and cities' dependency on land sales for revenue to finance urban development on the other hand.

2) Resources *and* pollution: Demand for resources from urban China will double. Water use is very likely to be a severe challenge with most water consumption still in agriculture.

3) Labor *and* skills: China will experience a shortage of skilled labor and talent, which is a serious threat to its aspiration to move quickly toward increasingly higher-value-added economic activity.

4) Funding: Providing services in cities will be more costly, while funding will be more difficult, especially with the enforcement of the policy for tighter restrictions on additional land acquisitions by the central government.

China would require holistic policy actions both at the national and the local levels, to increase overall efficiency and productivity of the urban system. Its resources would need to be mostly allocated for working toward a more economically developed and socially balanced society.

INDIA ON THE MOVE WITH RISKS OF A POLICY VACUUM

India is on the move, with its young and rapidly growing population, and the country needs to capitalize on its demographic potential. Cities are already of importance to India, with 340 million people (30 percent of the total population) living in urban India in 2008. It has been projected that the urban population will reach 590 million (40 percent of the total) by 2030.

The McKinsey Global Institution report indicates that India does not seem to realize the huge managerial and policy challenges that the speed of urbanization poses. There is little or no national discussion about how to handle this significant shift. India is still debating whether urbanization is positive or negative and whether the future lies in its villages or cities. MGI sees this dichotomy as non-existent, arguing that villages and cities are interdependent and symbiotic. Not paying attention to India's cities would cost the country tremendously in the future. Lack of policy today poses the risks of worsening urban decay and gridlock. The declining quality of life for citizens likely will cause reluctance among investors to commit resources to India's urban centers.

MGI recommends that India spend $2.2 trillion on cities over the next 20 years. The strategy for city development would make Tier1 and Tier2 cities nearly self-sufficient while giving additional support to weaker Tier3 and Tier4 cities from the central and state governments, at least $20 per capita per year. The country would need to work toward improving governance, facilitating distributed urbanization, and providing affordable housing.

There is reverse migration in India. The globalization of Bangalore and Hyderabad, in India, offers opportunities that have been drawing skilled immigrants homeward. Interestingly, the two cities have neither the density of financial and business headquarters nor the cultural excellence of truly global cities.

They are, however, worldwide leading cities by being connected to a world network of Indian expatriates, particularly through their information technology firms and their transnational workers.

There are nearly 53 million people (about 14% of India's urban population) who live in the three 10 million plus urban agglomerations. Another 9% of the urban population (32 million people), is in cities of sizes ranging between 5 and 10 million. A massive 27% of its total urban population (about 101 million people) dwells in cities between 500 thousand and 5 million in size. About half of the urban population (181 million people) resides in small towns with less than half a million people. The MGI report also says that the rate of growth of urbanization is slowing down.

LATIN AMERICA URGENTLY NEEDS TO TRANSFORM ITS URBAN ECONOMIES

The MGI study of Latin America (August 2011) found that it is more urbanized than any other region in the developing world, with 80 percent of its relatively young population living in cities. The 260 million people who currently live in its 198 large cities are projected to reach 315 million by 2025, more than the US population today. The cities will contribute 65% of the growth by 2025, when 50 million people are projected to enter the potential workforce.

Latin America's urban population has grown substantially due to people moving from the countryside to town. The region's 198 large cities contribute over 60 percent of their GDP today. Such concentration of urban economic activity is comparable with the

U.S and Western Europe today but it is much more concentrated than in any other emerging region.

Today housing shortages, traffic congestion, and pollution pose problems for many of Latin America's largest cities. To sustain their growth, they need to deal with challenges to their economic performance, their citizens' quality of life, sustainable resource use, the strength of their finances, and governance.

The relatively young population of Latin America makes transforming its urban economies urgent. Policy makers, businesses, and social societies in Latin America need to act to create more productive jobs to prevent the region from growing old before growing wealthy.

CONSEQUENCES OF URBANIZATION

Some metropolises like Los Angeles, sprawl outwards, consuming precious land through massive streets and transport systems. Little can be done to change Los Angeles' enormous spread with its substantial travel time in the automobile which is the major cause of pollution. The sprawling cities, with their road systems that cover hundreds of miles, often are built over land that is fertile and could otherwise be cultivated. Certainly, the outlying industries and their polluting activities often extend to the surrounding land and water. How can a city, that has such sprawl, be designed in a way that offers people private residences with gardens, while at the same time saving their health, recovering time lost in transportation, and decreasing the money spent on cars, and at the same time offering an accessible cultural and social life for those who want it?

Other metropolises, like New York, spread upwards. Its piecemeal growth has obstructed its functions and its separate territories have compartmented its life. Manhattan represents the way life in the upward city is perceived. Skyscrapers cast long shadows over roads and buildings; avenues and streets crisscross in a never-ending web, with elevated passages between buildings, there are subway entrances and subways, railroad stations, bus terminals and airports; and roads lead in and out of the city through tunnels and bridges. Life seems to be spent in moving from building to building. Everybody is doing the same thing at the same time of day: working, playing and resting. The pollution, congestion, and excessive hustle and bustle make it difficult for anyone to be aware of anything except managing to "get there" wherever that may be. Late in the night, city life quiets down; now the streets and office buildings are empty, and the apartments and houses are full and still. Turning to the living conditions, consider the energy consumed in heating and cooling the city, its water shortages, its scattered sewage plants polluting the rivers and the ocean, and the nearby garbage dumps and junk yards. What they need is better planning and design of their mega structures.

Urbanization drives transformations of landscapes and ecosystems, which in a situation of a rapid growing population might create the most challenging global environmental problems. It causes significant land use/land cover change and is recognized as one of the most important anthropogenic influences on climate. Given that there is a strong link between population, environment and development, land use and land cover analysis have environmental implications at both the local and regional levels. The land use/land cover is also linked to global environmental processes due to the interrelated relationship of elements within the natural environment, i.e., the direct effects on one element may cause indirect effects on others.

Global change has been a worldwide focus for governments, international organizations, and scientists in recent years. According to the 4th Assessment Report of the Intergovernmental Panel on Climate Change (IPCC), the global average surface temperature increased by 0.74°C over the last 100 years (1906-2005), and was caused mainly by human activities. If the current global change trend continues, it will have a tremendous impact on global ecosystems, particularly the estuary ecosystems. Research on global climate change, including assessments of its vulnerability and response strategies, suggests that land-use decisions and infrastructure investments should bear in mind the need to reduce vulnerability and enhance opportunities for urban populations.

One of the most well-known adverse effects induced by urbanization is the so-called "urban heat island" effect. Urban areas generally have higher solar radiation absorption and a greater thermal capacity and conductivity so that heat is stored during the day and released at night. As such, urban areas tend to experience relatively higher temperatures when compared with surrounding rural areas.

Given their population density and high investments in infrastructure and buildings, there is the potential for cities to suffer the consequences of climate change impacts. As cities, states, and nations undertake efforts to reduce and regulate greenhouse gas emissions, the concept of urban metabolism provides a framework for monitoring, reporting, and verifying that allows us to account for imports, exports, and transformations of carbon within urban areas.

Urbanization processes have created metropolitan areas that are heterogeneous urban systems in many respects, e.g., demographically, socio-economically, and environmentally. They are also heterogeneous in the ways they are impacted by, and respond to, climate change. Climate variability and change impact water availability, forcing the development of new adaptive measures. Although water availability is affected by climate change, water access is governed by social factors.

The costs have risen with the pressure to clean up the environment and with the shortage of cheap forms of energy. Human and environmental or habitat problems have run up against each other. To leave the city for nature is a thing so difficult, expensive, and time-consuming that few people think of doing it. One-fourth of all energy used in our society is consumed by transportation, the bulk of which occurs in the city where millions of vehicles move short distances many times a day. The total mileage of short distances of commuting is astronomical and uses a tremendous amount of energy.

According to the US Department of Energy, almost 40% of energy consumption can be attributed to buildings. Energy consumption depends on the age of the building, its architecture design, construction, use, and demolition. Studies also indicate that there is a connection between land use characteristics (type of housing, single/multi-family housing, size and age of housing, density) and household consumption of energy and transport. The difference in energy use for housing between single family and multifamily housing is reduced in those built after 1980. Energy consumption is also affected by proximity to mass transport and workplaces.

Congested cities are fast becoming test tubes for scientists studying the impact of traffic fumes on the brain. An article in the Wall Street Journal on November 8, 2011, reported that scientists increasingly link vehicle exhaust with brain-cell damage and higher rates of autism. Cars and trucks today generate one tenth the pollution of a vehicle in 1970. Still, more people are on the road and they are stuck in traffic more often. Drivers traveling the 10-worst U.S. traffic corridors annually spend an average of 140 hours, or about the time spent in the office in a month, idling in traffic.

Today urban living is on the rise, developing inner richness in those who experience it. Art museums, sports stadiums, music halls, and shopping malls thrive, indicating that cities and civilization are inseparable. A great city should handle both its garbage and its richness equally well.

While at first men lived closer simply to survive, they now live together because of the excitement and enjoyment they bring to each other. Most of the social and cultural amenities of a large city, however, are not easily accessible to its population. A city that has a smaller population of one-half to one million can still support many of these desirable activities and also make them more accessible.

Figure 1-1 (Source:
http://www.bloombergbusinessweekthailand.com/wp-content/uploads/2012/10/shopping-mall.jpg)

A city is an arena for creativity and appreciation where men's talents grow and potentials materialize. In cities, men invented machines to exploit in agriculture, causing shrinkage in the number of people in farming throughout the world. As machines do the work of hundreds of men in farms, the men have been released from their labor and have moved to the city, crowding it and demanding a new livelihood from its multidimensional activities. The city grew, and prosperity brought about suburban living, where people had the dual advantage of proximity to the city and its life, and of a rural living environment.

If there will be more cities and more city life, the question is: what kind of city and what kind of life? The Industrial Revolution brought more people to the city and its activities increased and diversified. Tents and mud huts grew to hamlets and villages, and the villages grew into towns. Then, a town grew to a city and the city became a metropolis. The metropolis became a megalopolis and the megalopolis became an ecumenopolis. The word Ecumenopolis (derived from the Greek οικουμένη, from the word meaning world, and πόλις (polis) meaning city, and thus meaning a city made of the whole world: *ecumenopolises* or *ecumenopoleis*) was invented in 1967 by the Greek city planner Constantinos Doxiadis. But perhaps a strong consideration should be to limit a city's size to improve its functions and the quality of its services it provides to its people.

The city now has a large number of people who must adapt to its life and who may not have the skills necessary for survival. When there is a contrast of the very poor and the rich, the gap between the haves and the have-nots may cause crime to emerge. Such a less favorable condition might trigger those who have the money to leave, depriving the city of their resources so that it cannot continually rejuvenate itself. Most cities today are losing housing and population, especially in the middle and upper income brackets. This is leaving the city with a population that demands more in services than its revenue can provide.

The world's poorest peoples and places are exposed to the greatest risks of global environmental change impacts. People in developing countries are most vulnerable to the increasing frequency and severity of extreme weather events, such as storm surges, droughts, floods, heat waves, and hurricanes, as well as the semi-permanent or permanent effects of sea-level rise, land subsidence or desert encroachment. Global population and demographic analysis indicate that cities in developing countries are growing in size and number without having the capacity to support the urban poor, who largely live in slums and informal settlements.

The inevitable increase in the urban share of total population can also have its advantages. Despite the current concentration of poverty, slum growth, and social disruption in cities, significant economic growth and urbanization in the industrial age are two sides of the same coin. Cities concentrate poverty but at the same time they also provide the best hope of escaping from it. Modern civilization damages the environment, but cities have the potential to have long-term sustainability. Cities create problems, but at the same time they also contain the solutions. The potential benefits of urbanization far outweigh the disadvantages.

Unlike their rural counterparts, cities offer opportunities for being hubs that contribute to economic growth, community building, and cultural creativity and expression. Concentrating human activities in urban centers can also protect habitats and increase the efficiency of municipal services. In contrast, however, poverty, crime, social detachment and pollution can increase in cities. The environmental impact of cities might be considered local, but the footprints of cities are extensive and can lead to widespread environmental degradation. These opportunities and problems present key challenges for improving urban living in a way that supports long-term growth and environmental as well as social sustainability.

Addressing the important and immediate concerns, such as improving living conditions of the poor, generating employment, ecological footprint, and administering increasingly complex urban systems, is not enough. The government's capability for urban planning, policy designing, and implementation is crucial.

The problem is that the growth in urban areas includes huge numbers of poor people, and the bulk of the population growth is likely to be in smaller cities and towns. The worldwide process of decentralizing governmental powers is accumulating greater responsibility for local authorities, whose capabilities for dealing with the issue can be very weak.

We cannot leave all the responsibility to deal with the urban expansion in the hands of the respective local governments only. Population, institutions, and specialists can and should also play a key role in supporting non-governmental community organizations, social movements, and the international community in improving the nature and form of future urban expansion. The power and capability to reduce poverty and promote environmental sustainability need to be enhanced. An international collaboration effort at this critical time is crucial to clarify policy options and provide information and analyses that support strategies to improve the future of our urban life. Most megacities support some level of civil society participation in the planning and design of their services, such as citizen involvement in the urban planning process.

THE NEED FOR HOLISTIC CITY GOVERNANCE

Administrations in large cities are often confronted with a multitude of key problems like high urban densities, transport, traffic congestion, energy inadequacy, unplanned development and lack of basic services, illegal construction both within the city and in the periphery, informal real estate markets, creation of slums, poor natural hazard management in overpopulated areas, crime, water, soil and air pollution, climate change, and poor governance arrangement. Some cities reported that their administrations have little control over their population growth, even in monitoring the change effectively to respond appropriately to the big challenges. Many cities also have problems with unclear and overlapping responsibilities among their internal and external agencies, leading to operational dysfunctions. Sao Paolo, Brazil, for example, is comprised of separate component cities, all with their own governance arrangement.

Informal settlements are a problem in many cities. An increasing number of citizens have neither permanent nor temporary access to land and adequate shelter. In many cases this is caused by structural social inequalities, inheritance constraints, or administrative systems that are ineffective and expensive. It requires a range of appropriate interventions within the broader context of economic growth and poverty reduction policies to prevent social exclusion and poverty from growing. Natural hazards and emergency management are major issues in most cities. Risk profiles and floods, fires, earthquakes, and other hazards differ among cities, but having the capacity to plan, prepare, and recover from disasters is a common need.

It is clear that solutions to problems facing megacities require collaborative response from their many internal units as well as from regional and national agencies in planning infrastructure development and land use controls, transportation, environmental aspects and water management. Mandates might be clear, but clear delineations of functions, more effective cooperation, and information sharing are needed.

Even if city planning is centrally coordinated, city administrations often have little control over the implementation of their policies and plans. For example, the greater Paris region in France has a regional planning authority that establishes planning policies for its highly decentralized 1,280 communes. Political differences create tensions in the implementation of those policies.

The influence of megacities reaches well beyond their administrative boundaries; it is essential that the greater region be managed holistically to maximize the economic benefits of the city. Regional planning not only requires effective governance of the larger region, but also across international boundaries, with cooperation in planning, development control, and information sharing being important. In many cases infrastructure providers are not a direct part of the city administration's planning and development process; some are private enterprises while others may be located at another level of government. This causes problems with proactive planning and the strengthening of city services.

We have been used to living with ready access to a multitude of material goods and services. Despite the problems of possible shortages and high costs of energy, we can move forward through a more judicious use of our resources.

Chapter 2

The Sustainable City

INTRODUCTION TO THE SUSTAINABLE CITY

The term *Sustainable Cities* has become important and attracted worldwide interest because the urban rapid growth causes severe economic, environmental, and social problems. It is increasingly difficult to manage this growth in a sustainable way, especially given that much growth currently takes place in an informal and organic way. There is worldwide concern with the idea of sustainability. In the mid 1990's this author was invited to Naples Italy by its mayor to show how decision making can be applied to improve city futures and city sustainability. In the early 1970's the government of Tanzania invited this author with a colleague to determine the best company to choose to move the capital from Dar es Salam on the sea to Dodoma, in the middle of the country, which is now the legislative capital, similar to Brazilia in the 'middle' of Brazil.

Wikipedia's definition of a sustainable city or eco-city is "a city designed with consideration of environmental impact, inhabited by people dedicated to minimization of required inputs of energy, water and food, and waste output of heat, air pollution – CO_2, methane, and water pollution." In addition to cutting down greenhouse gases, energy, water, waste, and other resources, attention needs to be given as well to any possible impact of bio-diversity.

Sustainability ultimately means efficiency: being as productive as possible with minimal waste. This has led to innovations like reducing packaging or selling toilet paper without cardboard rolls in the middle. What's most encouraging for environmental activists about this initiative is the vast size and power, and the ripple effect a sustainability program could have on the global economy. If the world's most influential corporation for building new cities is taking sustainability seriously, even for self-interested reasons, it has the power to affect real change in a way that only governments have previously been able to do.

At the same time, true sustainability isn't just about picking low-hanging fruit like excess packaging. It requires serious upfront investment in new technologies and other efforts that would likely lead to higher prices for consumers. And while environmental groups like the Environmental Defense Fund have gotten on board critics see the program as a halfhearted publicity stunt.

Sustainability is now the key driver of innovation and a key factor for business to be competitive. Products are to be developed with sustainability at the core of their design, so in education, sustainability is now an integral part of many curricula. Studies strongly support compact city as a sustainable urban form. Copenhagen, Denmark's capital has been declared as Europe's most eco-friendly city by the Economist Intelligence Unit in cooperation with Siemens, as confirmed by the European Green City index.

The need to make cities and communities sustainable has been championed by governments and non-governmental organizations as well as by companies developing technology solutions for urban living. However, the demand for technology and for services does not seem to grow fast enough for companies to justify investment in them.

Humanity needs and uses what nature provides. Ensuring sustainability requires us to balance our demands on nature with the rate of nature's capacity to regenerate. According to the Global Footprint Network (www.footprintnetwork.org), "It measures how much land and water area a human population requires to produce the resource it consumes and to absorb its carbon dioxide emission, using prevailing technology.

Our current global situation: since the 1970s humanity has been in ecological overshoot with annual demand on resources exceeding what the Earth can regenerate each year. It now takes the Earth one year and six months to regenerate what we use in a year."

Conversation among global urban innovators during the Partnership for Urban Innovation Global Conference in Shanghai on 17 June 2010 concluded that there are seven following constraints on sustainability.

1) Lack of metrics, processes, and tools;

2) Limited access to resources/best practices (employee skill sets, sustainability innovations);

3) Resistance from the private sector;

4) Lack of interest from citizens or unwillingness to change behavior;

5) Bureaucracy or lack of consensus among different stakeholders;

6) Unclear business case for sustainability investments;

7) Lack of funding.

Generally, urbanization assumes a horizontal sprawl with no concern for how population will increase the squandering of agricultural land. Andrew D. Basiago, a lawyer, writer and 21st century visionary, studied in the 1990's how to make cities sustainable and found that history suggests the following 15 general principles of sustainable urbanization. We found Basiago's work very useful and interesting to summarize these ideas about future cities and we often quote from it. Thus essentially we would be reporting on what Basiago says about different kinds of cities and often quoting him.

THE SUSTAINABLE CITY IS A GARDEN CITY THAT INTEGRATES TOWN AND COUNTRY (HOWARD, 1902)
Current study indicates that access to a private garden seems to reduce a residents' desire to travel in their leisure time, therefore saving energy. Sir Ebenezer Howard asked back in late 1800s: "How can we design cities that combine the best of town and country living?" The question launched the era of the 'Garden City', according to Howard, that would "combine all the economic and social advantages of an energetic and active town life with all the beauty and delight of the country". Howard's idea of 'Garden City' was born during the early era of the Industrial Revolution, which had created urban overcrowding and produced slums in many great cities. 'Garden City' has been remembered more for

its land use perspective rather than for its financial implication. His concept of a garden city is circular in form with a circular garden at its center.

Howard hoped that his proposal would trigger an international effort to build up clusters of beautiful hometowns, each zoned by gardens, for those who now dwell in crowded, slum cities. He saw town and country acted as magnets, but there were tradeoffs involved. The jobs, high wages, and life advancement of town attract people, but they are undermined by high rents and costs. Social opportunity and amusement are reduced by excessive hours, social isolation, and long commuting distances. Country living provides beauty and wealth but lacks society and capital. Rents in the country are low, but only because wages are. Its bright sunshine and pure air are diminished by lack of amusements. Drinking water, sanitation, and proper drainage are poor for lack of rural infrastructure.

Howard hoped that his proposal would trigger an international effort to build up clusters of beautiful hometowns, each zoned by gardens, for those who now dwell in crowded, slum cities. He saw town and country acted as magnets, but there were tradeoffs involved. The jobs, high wages, and life advancement of town attract people, but they are undermined by high rents and costs. Social opportunity and amusement are reduced by excessive hours, social isolation, and long commuting distances. Country living provides beauty and wealth but lacks society and capital.

Figure 2-1 Hydroponic sustainability (source:
http://hydroponicaccess.com
/wp-content/uploads/2010/10/garden3.jpg)

Rents in the country are low, but only because wages are. Its bright sunshine and pure air are diminished by lack of amusements. Drinking water, sanitation, and proper drainage are poor for lack of rural infrastructure.

Howard introduced the fundamental principle of sustainability by emphasizing the integration of town and country, the conservation of agricultural land, and the gradual movement of population away from crowded centers. His site plan causes low environmental impact. As the city grows, the free gifts of nature such as fresh air and sunlight would be retained.

THE SUSTAINABLE CITY POSSESSES THE VITAL FORM OF THE MEDIEVAL CITY (GEDDES, 1915)

Medieval cities possessed well planned streets and open spaces, beautiful and roomy dwellings and admirable public monuments that anchored the life of the community. They nurtured a healthy democratic civic life, providing public access to green belt for recreation, defending woodland and wetland and protecting the purity of the water supply. Sir Patrick Geddes showed how the successive stages of warfare and constructions for defense purposes, centralization, regionalization and industrialization, had destroyed the vital form of the medieval city. He maintains that the sustainability of cities and the quality of human life are closely interlinked. Geddes' concern is reflected today in the debate over open space. It is a quest to both restore the environment and revitalize human life, which requires a holistic approach.

THE SUSTAINABLE CITY HAS A FORM NEAREST TO ORGANIC AS POSSIBLE (WRIGHT, 1935)

Wright followed Howard's quest to free humans from overcrowded urban centers and return them to the country with its simpler rural society. He and his fellows created the idea of a new community called "Broadacre City" that had the following key elements: integrated decentralization, utilitarian land tenure, municipal property ownership, private home ownership, full employment, and small scale artisanship. The land would be held only for use and improvements; public utilities and the government would be "owned" by the people; and privacy would be protected. The city would use structures in forms as organic as possible. The idea was considered as a radical democratic vision.

Broadacre City was a concept of a city of small farms, small factories, small homes, small schools, and small workshops. They would be the setting of a culture based on independent artisanship and small scale collaboration. A new form of monetary exchange would be based on social credit, and the public would own the patent of new inventions. Many dimensions of Broadacre City persist in sustainable urbanization to this day. Wright knew the many benefits of urban forestry, which today is seen as fundamental to any sustainable town plan. His insistence that housing be available for people of different income levels persists in contemporary sustainability. Another attribute was local sufficiency through production at or near the place of consumption.

Basiago argued, however, that many aspects of Broadacre City were clearly not sustainable. The low density called for in the plan is inconsistent with the notion that urban compactness conserves land and allows preservation of habitat. Wright's idea was that the only popular fuels in the City would be non-renewable oil and gas, which are not sustainable. The idea of using copper roofs may be artistic but showed little understanding of energy conservation. His idea in transport was the least sustainable. His scheme of a mix of sustainable and non-sustainable elements leads to suburban sprawl and to eight-lane expressways. This neither leads to a sustainable city nor to a compact city.

THE SUSTAINABLE CITY ELEVATES THE MATERNAL, LIFE NURTURING FUNCTIONS (MUMFORD, 1938, 1961)

Lewis Mumford argued that a sustainable city is an urban form that would sustain the human spirit. He followed Howard's and Geddes's ideas, urging the adoption of a regional planning paradigm that would foster humane values, an urbanization era of the Biotechnic City. In the Biotechnic age, people would reject mechanistic and dehumanizing forms. He viewed Biotechnic as an urban form that is small, rural, kindly, pleasant, and cheerful, as well as integrated. He described Wright's architecture as a microcosm of the new Biotechnic economy, showing the way to the Biotechnic City by synthesizing nature and machine with human activities and purposes. Compactness and integration would allow the countryside to keep the active, dynamic elements of city life.

Food would be grown close to the urban market. The appropriate locations of factories and workshops would give agricultural families alternative occupations, making the use of land more productive. Consumption and service are more important than production for sale and profit. Consumption would be directed towards the conservation and improvement of life. He maintains that city population should be limited to between 25,000 and 50,000 citizens.

THE SUSTAINABLE CITY IS DESIGNED WITH NATURE (MCHARG, 1969)

Ian McHarg addressed the long lasting question of the era of ecological city: What is the place of nature in the world of humanity? A new form of city would be designed to work with nature and not against it. This question was followed by a practicable question: Where are the best places for cities? Planning should not merely address economic considerations, but the implications of development of physical, biological, and social processes.

Figure 2-2 (Source: http://www.visualphotos.com)

McHarg introduced a method to express both social and natural processes as social values. His method began by evaluating and ranking lands, tidal flood, historic, scenic, recreation, water, forest and wildlife, residential and institutional values for a given area. These values are each portrayed graphically on transparencies. The individual maps are then overlaid, forming a composite. This composite represents the sum of social values, physiographic opportunities and constraints. The optimum location to develop is identified with a view to incurring the least natural and social costs and create new social values. The most economical place on earth to develop is where it will be least destructive to nature's seamless web. His system is uniquely suited to regional planning based on water catchment boundaries.

Once the optimum place to urbanize is identified, the second major focus of his emerging design philosophy is to make cities self-sufficient. Cities that are resource and water efficient and store resources locally will last longer if supplies are interrupted. Designing cities to use local resources creates sustainability, e.g., by requiring solar cells on roofs and the recycling of sewage to grow food, materials and crops. It makes regions less vulnerable to disaster, creates jobs and saves money on imports.

Figure 2-3 (Source: http://growingplantsindoors.com/wp-content/uploads/2010/04/madridmainstation.jpg)

THE SUSTAINABLE CITY IS A PERMACULTURE (MOLLISON, 1978)
Bill Mollison saw that societies with permanent agricultural systems have achieved permanent cultural systems. Permaculture is an urban design strategy over time that integrates community patterns with ecological necessities. The

key to permaculture is to understand that its design is based on nature's own systems. It identifies the energy 'source' and the energy 'sink', and then defines how they work together. Founded in the simple analysis of basic energy, food, water, and nutrient needs, permaculture holds the potential to reduce demand on utilities and supermarkets.

THE SUSTAINABLE CITY FEATURES SOLAR DESIGN, NATURAL DRAINAGE, EDIBLE LANDSCAPE (M. CORBETT AND J. CORBETT, 1984)

Begun in 1975 in the wake of the first oil crisis, the California community Village Homes characterizes ecological city by featuring solar architecture, a pedestrian friendly layout, natural drainage, and edible landscape. Planned as a model of sustainable development, Village Homes commercialized sustainability. It has been shown that when residential development implements sustainable principles, both economic and environmental benefits follow.

THE SUSTAINABLE CITY IS COMPACT AND REGENERATIVE OF DAMAGED OR DERELICT URBAN LAND (CEC, 1990)

The European Commission (EC)'s urban Green Paper endorses environmental and economic sustainability in its city revitalization strategy. The recommendation adopts two principal approaches in contemporary urban sustainability: revitalizing cities by making them more compact and regenerating existing urban land. The EC recommended that something of the heterogeneity, physical beauty, and compactness of historic cities be restored. People would be brought closer to their jobs and daily services. The EC linked solving the problems of cities with solving world environmental problems such as global warming and acid rain.

THE SUSTAINABLE CITY IS MADE COMPACT TO ALLOW SURROUNDING WILDERNESS TO FLOURISH (NASH, 1991)

Robert Nash sees urban compactness as an essential element of sustainability. For the next millennium, Nash envisioned an 'Island Civilization' of 1.5 billion humans living in 500 concentrated cities of three million people. Integrated into each of these cities would be the means to produce food, water, energy, and materials. Wilderness conditions would be returned as species roamed vast spaces of habitat between the 500 cities. Nash's 'Island Civilization' would be highly technologically advanced, reaching 1.6 km in height, and would be built above and below ground, at sea and at poles. Highly compact and highly self-sufficient technopoles would allow all water, electricity, and transportation between existing cities to be dismantled. Habitats located in the 48 American states would occupy no more than 2 percent of America soil.

Nash writes that his 'Island Civilization' would serve four objectives. First, it would allow the human presence on earth to endure for many thousands of years. Second, it would advance the rights of nature by curtailing the extinction of species and the loss of vital habitat. Third, it would preserve wilderness between cities to instruct humans on the functioning of healthy ecosystem. Lastly, it would allow the global population to maximize theirs.

THE SUSTAINABLE CITY HAS A CIRCULAR METABOLISM (GIRARDET, 1992)

Herbert Girardet argued that compactness alone will not lead to sustainability. A city with a high population density surrounded by wildlife habitat is wasteful. He distinguishes the 'circular metabolism' of sustainable cities from the 'linear metabolism' of modern cities. In the 'linear metabolism' of modern cities, the imported natural resources are converted to waste in a wasteful input-output pattern. To be sustainable, urban metabolism must be made 'circular' with plant nutrient recycling based on food production. Needed are clean and maximum efficient energy technology, recycled materials, and large scale tree planting.

THE SUSTAINABLE CITY MAKES NO WASTE, SEEKS BIODIVERSITY, RELIES ON THE SUN (MCDONOUGH, 1992)

William McDonough addresses the process of sustainability, believing that achieving a sustainable civilization is a design problem. A new industrial order will have to be built. He urges designers to insist on the rights of humanity and nature to coexist in a healthy, supportive, diverse, and sustainable condition. For sustainability to emerge, designers must accept responsibility for the consequences of design decisions upon human wellbeing, the viability of natural systems, and their right to coexist and create only safe objects of long term value. Future generations are not to be burdened with requirements for maintenance or to be watchful of potential danger due to the careless creation of products, processes, or standards. In nature there is no waste, hence it is important to eliminate the concept of waste from industry. The principles also state that human design should derive their creative forces from everlasting solar income like the living world.

The new industrial order will be guided by the following three principles of nature.

1) Nature produces only food, no waste;

2) Nature promotes maximum diversity;

3) Nature relies on its solar energy account. Solar energy would be the primary energy of civilization.

THE SUSTAINABLE CITY DOES NOT EXCEED NATURE'S CARRYING CAPACITY (CANFIELD, 1993)

Cerro Gordo in Oregon, a town of 2500, was based on a study of the carrying capacities of the valley in which it is located. Two dozen environmental factors and intrinsic land use suitability were examined. The site most suitable for the village center (as indicated by 24 factors) was abandoned to preserve a major wildlife corridor. The town also was inspired by the notion of symbiotic community, bringing together village, farm and forest. Cerro Gordo and towns like it reversed the depletion and destruction of natural support systems, i.e., conversion (to industry manufacturing non-toxic, non-destructive, and non-exploitative products only), conservation (the reuse, reduction, and recycling of resources), renewable energy (e.g., solar), regeneration (the re-growth of natural support systems, and symbiosis (defined as partnership, qualitative growth, and co-evolution).

THE SUSTAINABLE CITY USES TRANSIT ORIENTED DEVELOPMENT TO CONTROL GROWTH (CALTHORPE, 1993)

Posing a question "What qualities make a city sustainabile?" the 'New Urbanism' is more of a community than a natural feature. It calls for creating new community space that is dense, diverse, and convenient. Peter Calthorpe's model contains dense town centers built around transit stops. He argued that it would not possible to preserve nature in smaller urban parcels. The Transit-Oriented-Development (TOD) becomes a framework for controlling regional growth.

THE SUSTAINABLE CITY IS HOLISTIC, DIVERSE, FRACTAL, AND EVOLUTIONARY (MCDONALD, 1994)

The work of Margot McDonald and colleagues is considered as one of the most sophisticated models of contemporary sustainable urbanism. They were invited to propose ideas for sustainable built environment that would affect building design, architectural technologies, and community development over the next 50 to 100 years. The ideas would have to fit their physical and socio-economic context and be technically feasible. Most importantly, they would have to improve local and global sustainability both socially and ecologically.

They formed four performance criteria to compare and evaluate solutions for the implementation of any sustainable community design. First, a sustainable urban system is holistic, comprising interdependent and interconnected subsystems at multiple scales. Second, a sustainable urban system is diverse. Decisions should enhance biological, social, cultural, and economic diversity at all scales. Third, a sustainable urban system is fractal. A fractal system is composed of interested and interacting systems whose fundamental qualities, processes, and physical forms appear self-similar at many scales. Fractal geometry is not merely a way to design with nature but it is like nature.

THE SUSTAINABLE CITY IS COMPRISED OF GREEN INFRASTRUCTURE (LYLE, 1994)

John T. Lyle believes that urban sustainability will only be achieved when society incorporates the regenerative energy and water flow systems of nature into its cities. In nature, the landscape supports life.

Figure 2-4 (Source: http://growingplantsindoors.com/wp-content/uploads/2010/04/chicagobotanicgardenwaterfall.jpg)

Solar energy is converted into usable forms. Food is produced and water is guided and purified. Waste is integrated. The sustainable city of the future is an urban form that would achieve a functional synthesis of urban systems and natural systems.

Basiago maintains that governing sustainable land use requires addressing these three issues:

1) It is necessary to find the optimal sites for urban and industrial activities. The location of the society's actual wealth (e.g., best agricultural soils) needs to be identified.

2) The financial system must adopt the cost accounting system of nature. True cost pricing accounts for the true environmental costs of a good or service, creating

economic incentives to seek environmentally beneficial alternatives.

3) Sustainable buildings must become the basic unit of urbanization. It must not causing sickness, is safe, is not built on a flood plain, conserves water, is surrounded by climatically suitable edible landscape, and relies on solar energy.

SUSTAINABLE TRANSPORTATION

Sustainable transportation is generally defined as satisfying current transportation and mobility needs without compromising the ability of future generations to meet their own needs. Criteria for sustainable transportation include:

1) Economic objectives, such as the extent of satisfying transportation demand and the technical as well as commercial feasibility of the transportation technology;

2) Environmental objectives, such as the production and regeneration functions;

3) Social objectives, such as cultural richness, institutional factors, and social equity.

The proposed key strategies on a general level (national, state, and regional level) that function as the regulatory framework toward sustainable transportation are:

1) Reduction of space consumption;

2) Concentration of development (compact city);

3) Reduction of motorized traffic;

4) Encouragement of alternative transportation modes, especially public transit systems;

5) Introduction of technology innovations to manage travel demand.

SOCIAL LIFE OF CITIES

Discussion about urban sustainability usually is focused on its economic and environmental dimensions, without addressing its social life. The main concern here is how to avoid the pattern of diminished communities, disconnected people, and depressing surroundings of the most modern parts of cities, and some of the most modern cities themselves.

The Urban Innovation Global Conference in Shanghai on 17 June 2010 also indicated that there are three distinct issues relating to the social life of cities. They involve:

1) Social life at work and looking at emerging patterns of working fuelled by new social networking tools and platforms that link work, home and community in new ways;

2) Examples of social innovation in the city and learning from a new breed of social entrepreneurs who are finding new ways to combine technology, culture, and people to solve difficult problems of isolation, intolerance, and inequity;

3) The creative life of cities including examples of approaches to creating cultural experience that engages as well as entertains.

The way people live, work, learn, and play in 21st century cities is different from what it was in the past. As a result, city designs and developments are becoming increasingly people-centric. The main question raised by global urban innovators is how people driven, technologically enhanced city design and development can transform urban life, the experience of "place" and real estate demand. These inquiries include:

1) How has the citizen experience of the city being enhanced?

2) What are trends in new city design to create connection, collaboration, and convenience? How is the resulting real estate impacted as cities transition to multipurpose, space on demand programmable entities?

3) How are these new cities disrupting traditional real estate uses of space?

4) What is the impact on the real estate business models and what are the resulting value propositions?

HEALTHCARE

A study by Lee et.al prioritizing wellbeing indices of super tall residential buildings in Korea indicated that health is most important, followed by safety and security, then the ecological environment. Function and management was considered to be the least important of all.

Health promotion movement has been developing rapidly after the joint International Conference of the World Health Organization (WHO) and the United Nations Children's Fund (UNICEF) on primary healthcare in 1978. They adopted the Alma-Ata declaration which gave the definition of primary health care and accepted it as an essential approach towards increasing health status, in addition to curative medicine. The global 'Health for All' strategy launched by the World Health Assembly in 1981 adopted the primary health care approach, a mix of essential health services, personal responsibility for one's own health, and health promotion activities.

The health problems facing the world today are increasingly complex, requiring interventions that are across all sectors and levels of organizations. Cities especially face challenging health conditions like obesity, avian flu, infant mortality, and depression as well as social conditions like concentrated poverty, rising inequality, and declining public infrastructures. To be effective, health promotion needs integrated efforts by the healthcare, education, environmental protection, housing, nutrition, and economic development sectors.

Who defines intersectoral health promotion intervention as organized activities that seek to improve well-being by influencing multiple determinants of complex health problems that operate across sectors and levels of organization? Sectors are functional areas such as education, employment, and health care; levels describe hierarchical arenas of social interaction such as individuals, families, communities, and jurisdictions. Intersectoral interventions make changes in different systems to achieve defined public health goals.

Intersectoral health promotion has the potential to contribute to solving a wide range of health problems. In some cases, healthcare receives unintended or secondary benefits of initiatives designed to achieve economic, educational, or other goals. This approach is particularly useful for addressing problems whose causes or consequences manifest themselves in different sectors. It is useful for addressing what have been called wicked problems that are resistant to solutions with categorical interventions. However, even relatively straightforward medical problems, e.g., tuberculosis, require interventions that address health care, water, housing, transportation, and employment. Solving complex problems often also require the participation of those constituencies who are affected by the problem. Intersectoral approaches bring these parties together to learn from their diverse perspectives.

There are three ways to link health objectives and sectoral involvement:

1) Identify a single health objective and work across sectors to achieve that goal;

2) Choose multiple health outcomes and work across sectors to achieve the goals;

3) Choose objectives that cut across sectors, requiring activities in different sectors to achieve different outcomes.

Case studies reported successful health promotion targeted to older population. The options available for encouraging senior citizens to get involved, and supporting them in their daily lives are numerous. The creativity as well as the commitment of the project coordinators and the resources available plays an important role in establishing a local action plan.

MILLENNIUM DEVELOPMENT GOALS (MDGS)

MDGs are the United Nations' approach to focus on the reduction of poverty and to specify global actions needed to overcome social problems. Eight cross-cutting goals are proposed. They are aimed at poverty and hunger, universal primary education, gender equality, child mortality, maternal health, HIV/AIDS and other diseases, environmental sustainability, and global partnership for development. How frontline and national public health professionals locate health promotion initiatives within the context of MDGs and how they respond to the progressive critics of the top-down MDG approach will play an important role in shaping the future of intersectoral health promotion.

Interventions with more objectives and operating in more sectors are more complex and require coordination in planning and allocating resources, as well as in implementing and evaluating the progress of the plan. One of the challenges is uniting sectors with different interests and end goals. Allowing for representatives of each relevant sector in the planning and evaluation process would be a way to work collaboratively on interventions whose objectives cut across several sectors.

SOCIETAL QUALITY OF LIFE (QOL)

Quality of life is not only an individual issue. It is also the concern of a group of individuals, be it a family, a community, or a society as a whole. It has been argued that research in QOL at the moment is too focused on individual-level happiness, which could be at the expense of the quality of life at the society level. The emergent concepts of societal QOL also address the most important issue: survival of the species. They need to be embraced as well. Enhancing societal QOL would include reducing negative survival features.

Individual happiness is important, and it has been argued that current research on the quality of life is too focused on individual-level happiness, at the expense of societal level quality of life. Although happiness of individuals is important to societal QOL, the emergent concepts of societal QOL also need to be embraced, addressing the most important issue: survival of the species. Enhancing societal QOL must include reducing the negative side of survival features such as suicide, homicides, wars, and terrorist intrusion.

The most macro issue of societal QOL is the good life in a good society. This involves norms and values, social equality, structural relationship, and other quality of societies. Examples of values are those related to sustainability and social cohesion, institutional integration as well as regulation by the government, positive family and inter-generational relations, charity and welfare to the poor, freedom, equality, and solidarity.

The good society is more than the sum of happiness of its citizens. M. Joseph Sirgy compiled the following list of some of the areas to be covered under social quality as an emergent concept; that should include institutional roles, infrastructures, and processes:

1) Provisioning of welfare;

2) Minimizing labor conditions that could exclude certain segments of society from reaping the benefits of provisioning;

3) Creating and maintaining social networks;

4) Helping people to realize their competencies to fully participate in the social, economic, political, and cultural milieu;

5) Promoting peace and security;

6) Eradicating plaques and pandemics;

7) Encouraging religious membership and tolerance;

8) Regulating population growth;

9) Addressing better health, the socialization of children, community and neighborhood, and leisure time.

SAFE CITIES: THREATS, TERRORISM, NATURAL DISASTERS, ENERGY, AIR, WATER, FOOD, WASTE PROBLEMS

One answer to terrorism might be hoarding bombs! There was a fool who carried a live bomb in his briefcase whenever he flew (the analogy: visited a large city). After a while, he was stopped by the authorities who asked him why he did it. "For my own safety," the fool replied. "One night, I calculated that the odds of someone carrying a bomb on an airplane (into a large city where I was) were 1 in 10,000. That frightened me, and I decided that I would never fly (visit the city) again. Then I realized that the odds of there being two live bombs on a plane (in a large city) were 1 in 50,000,000. And ever since then, I've always taken mine with me."

Security is becoming increasingly critical to the functionality of our daily tasks. The cities themselves, the industry, and the technology are the biggest drivers toward safer cities. The threat to the security of cities demands attention from local authorities and law environment services. It has changed the role of the city in social responsibility and the well-being of the citizens. City authorities are under enormous pressure to cope not only with the common, expected security threats but also with unexpected ones, including terrorism, floods, earthquakes, and other environmental issues. Mega Cities, in particular, are learning from this much quicker, since a small disruption in any of the city's infrastructure (e.g., energy supply, mass transportation) potentially affects millions of people and generates financial loss and security issues. Gradually, local authorities become increasingly important in promoting national security, a role that in the past has been limited to the federal government.

The defense and security industry pushes the concept of safe city. To the industry, safe city is a new set of customers with large number potential. Safe cities might be similar for defense companies to what they traditionally have been serving, but it might also be an entirely new environment. Defense companies will have to consider new business models, alliances, and alternative ways of creating value for potential customers. Security companies are more familiar with working with local authorities, but they need to bring their solution to a higher level to meet the expectation of the new safe city market. It requires integration and interoperability between security solutions and other infrastructures. Partnership with different sectors such as energy, construction, and transportation are likely to impact the way security organizations will enter this new market.

There are two aspects of a safe city project: a social and a technological intent. The social intent refers to the key objective of a safe city initiative to enhance the well-being of citizens, and the technological intent refers to the type of security and safety solutions that will enable city operators to promote well-being in an ever changing urban environment. Technology is another key driver in safe cities, providing security and safety solutions to detect, act, and manage potential threats. As technology evolves, it is likely that the current ideas surrounding safe cities will change to take advantage of technological innovations.

SMART CITIES

According to Wikipedia a smart city is characterized by a smart economy; smart mobility; a smart environment; smart people; smart living; and, finally, smart governance. Discussing the market for safe city technology addresses the question of how it relates to the creation of smart cities. A simple way of correlating these two concepts is by understanding their ultimate goals. Smart city initiatives aim to deploy technology solutions across different city infrastructures with very specific goals. For example, smart transportation solutions are deployed to optimize traffic flow, increase transport connectivity, reduce time spent on mobility, etc. Another example is smart energy technology to increase efficiency, reduce pollution across urban areas, and make use of renewable sources. In essence, the smart concept involves using cutting edge technologies and solutions to make a city a better place to live. "Safe" is the enabler of "smart" – they do not compete with each other.

Cities increasingly have more economic, political, and technological power than ever before. Operationally, there are a number of core systems in cities, composed of different networks, infrastructures, and environments related to their key functions: city services, citizens, business, transport, communication, water, and energy. These core systems are interconnected in a synergistic fashion, creating a 'system of systems'.

Each element of this 'system of systems' provides the potential for significant positive transformation. At the same time, it also faces significant sustainability challenges and threats. As cities face these substantial and interrelated challenges, cities must use their power to become smarter, using new technologies to transform their core systems to optimize use of limited resources.

Dr. Boyd Cohen, a climate strategist helping to lead communities, cities and companies on the journey towards the low carbon economy, has provided the following structure: (see http://www.fastcoexist.com/1680538/what-exactly-is-a-smart-city), that he calls the Smart Cities Wheel:

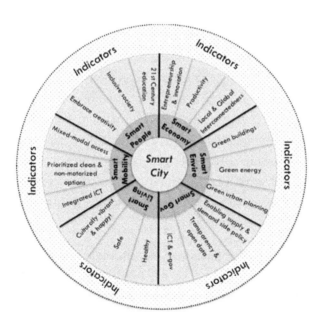

Figure 2-5 Dr. Boyd Cohen's smart cities wheel

Smarter cities present the opportunity for sustainable prosperity. Similar to the compact city idea, becoming a 'smarter city' is a journey of a *revolutionary*, not evolutionary, change. City administrations must decide what activities are core, by identifying those that they should discard, retain, or expand into. Cities must integrate their own administrations and work with other levels of government, especially country-level, as well as private and non-profit sectors. Cities must understand the interrelationships among the systems they are based on, as well as the interactions among the challenges they face.

DECISION MAKING: PREPARATION FOR THE GROWING URBANIZATION

The future of cities and the future of humanity itself, all depend very much on decisions made now in preparation for the growing urban population. It is a complex situation requiring holistic policy decisions with the need for making tradeoffs. For example, increasing urban population density requires use of the vertical dimension in city design and construction to conserve land use, conserve energy and other scarce resources, while maintaining the quality life in the cities which requires more open space and green environment.

The IBM Institute for Business Value has identified a number of key steps for major cities to follow, to plan continuous improvement for their systems and the overall quality of life and business they support. The essential stages of this 'smarter cities roadmap' are:

1) Develop your city's long term strategy and short term goals;

2) Prioritize and invest in a few, select systems that will have the greatest impact;

3) Integrate across systems to improve citizen experiences and efficiencies;

4) Optimize your services and operations;

5) Discover new opportunities for growth and optimization.

CHALLENGES TO DECISION MAKING IN URBAN DEVELOPMENT

The need for future cities arises because of the rapid growth in population, thereby causing a decline in living standards in existing cities. Today's cities are getting more and more crowded by the day and the continuing influx will make current cities unmanageable and unlivable. With increasing wealth, the average house size has almost doubled since 1970 and this has further caused the decline in arable land and in forests. To deal with the problem of rising population and congestion within the cities, we need to plan cities for the future that would be able to utilize the available resources in a more efficient and cleaner manner.

More population means faster consumption of natural resources in land, water, air and energy which eventually leads ecological imbalance. Already more than 80% of the world's forests are gone. To accommodate the population, approximately 2000 trees are cut every minute in the Amazon alone. Food consumption has also doubled over the last fifty years and this has exerted pressure on the landscape through the use of artificial fertilizers. The use of artificial agents to boost agricultural productivity has significantly marred the flora and fauna leading to the loss of a huge amount of bio diversity.

Buildings in a conventional city are rigid and expensive to alter or replace. What we build in a conventional city is what we are stuck with for several subsequent generations. Society pays a high price for inflexible, rigid construction that may be initially cheap. There is obviously a challenge in responding to the inevitable need for revolutionary rather than evolutionary redesign of a fast-growing cities given its cost consequences: to let it take its natural course and end up obsolete and very expensive to remedy, or sustain and improve its design and function.

Chapter 3

Why Compact City?

INTRODUCTION

Generally speaking, the interiors of the dwellings, shops, work facilities and schools within cities are becoming more pleasant places to be, not less so. But several aspects of city life have become dangerous, time consuming, inconvenient, expensive, and unpleasant. Everyone wants to be free of the urban pollution that one can directly sense: smoke, grime, litter, odors, city heat, din, poor water, and urban blight. But the environmental degradation associated with urban development can also be measured in terms of disrupted ecosystems and wasteful use of green space and natural resources. Our purpose will be directed towards a redesign of the urban environment so as to minimize these negative aspects and to preserve and to enhance the qualities of urban life that we and most of the world have come to accept as desirable.

We want to arrange the city so that it works better – so that neighborhoods become more lively, safe, and relevant for children; and so that the city itself becomes a more exciting center for personal interactions in today's fast-moving world. If we look into the distant future when the workings of the mind become our dominant enterprise, we see the city planned, designed, integrated and sustainable in the most efficient form. It uses the third dimension and uses nature as part of its art work rather than its dominant feature.

The term *Compact City* was first coined in 1973 by George Dantzig and Thomas L. Saaty two mathematicians whose utopian vision was largely driven by a desire to see more efficient use of resources and better survival for people in an environment bristling with energy. Urban intensification which increases population density will reduce per capita car use, with benefits to the global environment, but will also increase concentrations of motor traffic, worsening the local environment in those locations where it occurs. Some people like Le Groupe Esprit Campagne of France have interpreted the concept in terms of hotel-like activities of lodging and sleeping; simply a place to live and sleep that is compact.

Sustainable development has become increasingly significant as a target for creating a better future for the world, economically, socially and environmentally. A city may be sustainable but not considered great. In his article: What makes a great city great? An American, H. V. Savitch, begins by dealing with concepts that extrapolate and define city greatness, synthesized in a simple formulation of the "4Cs"; standing for, respectively: *currency* (a city's fundamental values and its ability to form, lead or dictate the temper of the time), *cosmopolitanism* (the city's ability to embrace international, multicultural or polyethnic features), *concentration* (demographic density and productive mass) and *charisma* (the magical appeal of a city that generates mass enthusiasm, admiration or reverence).

It is easier to apply these concepts to a compact city because it is all controlled by man and little attention has to be paid to the weather and other factors in designing and shaping its structure and functions.

Joshua Arbury of Auckland New Zealand, writes this about the compact city idea: "In recent years city planners, developers and policymakers have increasingly looked towards designing a more 'compact city' in order to achieve a more sustainable urban form. There are many perceived benefits of the compact city over 'urban sprawl', which include: less car dependency thus lower emissions, reduced energy consumption, better public transport services, increased overall accessibility, the re-use of infrastructure and previously developed land, a rejuvenation of existing urban areas and urban vitality, a higher quality of life, the preservation of green space, and the creation of a milieu for enhanced business and trading activities. About his idea of Compact city he writes: "I will argue that the compact city model is necessary, but not sufficient for sustainability," and "some aspects of intensification, in some places, have contributed to sustainability, whilst others have clearly not."

One characteristic of our time is the building of roads to handle the huge traffic both inside and outside cities. See the jammed highway in China in the picture above that consumes so much good land and cement and time from the people that use it. People cover more miles of distance commuting to work and doing chores in and around the city where they live than they do in traveling between cities. The amount of cement and concrete we use to build roads and highways can be used instead to build the cities of the future that should not have and do not need wide roads; these cities will have minimal roads, traffic and resulting congestion.

Figure 3-1 Traffic jam 60 miles long in Beijing, China, lasted 11 days

In their "Principles of Intelligent Urbanism" the Department of Urban Development and Engineering Services, Ministry of Works and Human Settlement, Royal Government of Bhutan, 2005, provides us with the following ten axioms for planning towns and cities:

1) *A balance with nature*; the necessary balance between utilizing resources and exploiting them.
2) *A balance with tradition*; intended to integrate planned interventions with existing cultural assets, respecting traditional practices and precedents of style. This urban

planning principle demands respect for the cultural heritage of a place.

3) *Appropriate technology*; emphasizes the employment of building materials, construction techniques, infrastructural systems and project management which are consistent with local contexts.

4) *Conviviality*; sponsors social interaction through public domains, in a hierarchy of places, devised for personal solace, companionship, romance, domesticity, "neighborliness," community and civic life: a place for the individual, a place for friendship, a place for householders, a place for the neighborhood, a place for communities, and a place for the city domain.

5) *Efficiency*; promotes a balance between the consumption of resources such as energy, time and fiscal resources, and planned achievements in comfort, safety, security, access, tenure, productivity and hygiene.

6) *Human scale*; Intelligent Urbanism encourages ground-level, pedestrian-oriented urban patterns, based on anthropometric dimensions. Walkable, mixed use urban villages are encouraged over single-function blocks, linked by motor ways, and surrounded by parking lots.

7) *Opportunity matrix*; envisions the city as a vehicle for personal, social, and economic development, through access to a range of organizations, services, facilities and information providing a variety of opportunities for enhanced employment, economic engagement, education, and recreation.

8) *Regional integration*; envisions the city as an organic part of a larger environmental, socio-economic and cultural-geographic system, essential for its sustainability.

9) *Balanced movement*; advocates integrated transport systems comprising walkways, cycle paths, bus lanes, light rail corridors, under-ground metros and automobile channels.

10) *Institutional integrity*; holds that good practices inherent in considered principles can only be realized through accountable, transparent, competent and participatory local governance, founded on appropriate data bases, due entitlements, civic responsibilities and duties.

The Bhutan Department also advocates intelligent urbanism that promotes opportunities through access to:

1) Basic and primary education, skill development and knowledge about the urban world;
2) Basic health care, potable water, solid waste disposal and hygiene;
3) Urban facilities like storm drainage, street lights, roads and footpaths;
4) Recreation and entertainment;
5) Transport, energy, communications;
6) Public participation and debate;
7) Finance and investment mechanisms;

8) Land and/or built-up space where goods and services can be produced;
9) Rudimentary economic infrastructure.

Intelligent urbanism provides a wide range of zones, districts and precincts where activities and functions can occur without detracting from one another. To begin with we put a certain amount of required of infrastructure in place "underground". The first "basement" story could be set aside for local traffic, navigating in a double-lane grid with roundabouts every few hundred meters. A grid structure would make it easier to find your way, given the lack of a view. When you have arrived at your destination you turn off into the garage near your chosen district and find a parking lot close to where you are going.

The roof structure of the first basement story could be partially open to let in light and air; for instance, by using gratings. At least some of the roundabouts should be opened up, so that the motorists can get a view of the landscape – both to get their bearings as well as to alleviate any claustrophobia.

Below this we may add two layers of motorways for long-haul traffic, as well as the subways. Note that the underground roads are not dug down into the ground – they are built at the ground level. The high-rise buildings are built with the necessary number of "basement" stories to get their "first floor" to be level with the pedestrianized streets. Motorways or subways may be dug into trenches below the "first basement floor".

Humans, animals and plants and combustion machines need oxygen 24 hours a day and seven days a week. In a world in which there are many people, animals, and smoking machines the oxygen becomes polluted, the atmosphere clouded with soot, thus raising the environmental temperature; all need to be controlled, and wearing breathing apparatus day and night is inconvenient. In addition, crowding has changed the architecture of our cities from villages to megalopolises. In New York, Paris, London, Shanghai or Singapore, buildings go up. There are so many buildings and so much traffic to commute from one skyscraper to another that these buildings themselves would be better by being integrated.

Usable land is becoming scarce as the population of the world edges up toward ten billion. The capacity of the earth to have enough arable land will be challenged. It takes nearly a thousand square miles of arable land to feed two million people and three and a half million square miles to feed the more than 7 billion people living today, an area equal to that of the entire United States, but the land should all be arable and the US figure includes mountains and desert. Much more land is needed to feed the 1.5 billion cows, 1.2 billion sheep, 1 billion pigs, 700 million goats, 160 million water buffalos, 16 billion chickens, 75 million horses, and 44 million donkeys in the world. There are in addition 72 million dogs and 2 billion cats requiring meat from the other grazing animals to live. Methane has a half-life of about 7 years in the atmosphere. Greenhouse gases are gases in earth's atmosphere that trap solar radiation and warm the atmosphere. In one year, 100 million cows emit about 5.5 million metric tons of methane gas, or 82.5 million tons for the 1.5 billion cows in the world The ubiquitous termites are suspect of methane pollution because their population explodes where forests have been burned off to create farm and grazing land. It is estimated that there are 4,400 termites per square yard in tropical forests and wet savannahs, their favorite natural habitat, six to seven thousand per square yard in burned off clearings. It has been estimated that these wood-chompers produce 150 million metric tons of methane a year worldwide.

There is a lot of land but it has to be cared for more and more. According to Wikipedia, the world's total arable land amounts to 13,805,153 km², with 48,836,976 km² being classified as "agricultural land." One square kilometer equals 247.1 acres and thus 14 million square kilometers equals 3.5 billion acres, so the arable land available in the world should be able to feed about 10 billion people. In 2050 there will be nearly that many people living. And there are more things, both aesthetic and practical, that have to be considered for people to live in an increasingly crowded world that is also subject to the hazards of nature.

There is no a priori reason why one should prefer open spaces to the modern metropolis of skyscrapers. But evolutionary trends led us to live closer together, most likely so we can share creativity and productivity. We are using our thinking brains to turn inward more and more today as we use our senses less and less to look outside. Our educational system and our electronic devices turn us inward away from the environment around us; even researchers of the environment eventually turn inward to interpret what they find.

Though our numbers are increasing we are moving from open to closed environments. Fewer people live on farms while the majority of people have moved to urban centers. There seems to be no reversing the trend of moving into closer spaces, so how can we structure and frame the environment in which we find ourselves, and which way are these trends moving? If one lives in Japan, Hong Kong, Singapore, England, France and Italy, and other great cities/countries with limited space their future will be determined by the ways the people find to live in beautiful closed cities.

The researcher, Chisato Takahashi, from Japan, writes, "Compact City is a breakthrough idea that may help us solve the urban sprawl problem along with high infrastructure investments due to de-population. It enables one to decrease the public burden such as high infrastructure expense by population concentration in the center of cities. Today, the idea of Compact City is really implemented in local cities. I evaluated the effectiveness of high rises and high density urban structure for realizing a compact city in Tokyo. It would generate more spare time for enjoying theatres or museums by living closer to the work place, and in the end community activities would be likely to increase as well."

ORCHARDS IN BLOOM

The story of exploding urban areas is a familiar one that is unfolding throughout the United States. Sir Patrick Geddes uses the term *conurbation* to describe the process whereby first unorganized settlements spot themselves along a main highway at some distance from a city; then, between the radiating highways, real estate interests develop a fine grid of "endless rows of little boxes or of larger boxes with picture windows," and finally there is the back flow of development which closes the gap between the suburbs and the city. Meanwhile the central city, weakened by the flow of its vitality to the suburbs, rots and turns to slums.

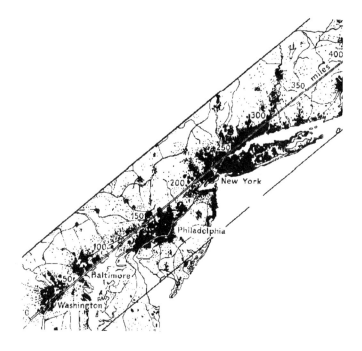

Figure 3-2 Megalopolis 400 miles long extending from south of Washington, D.C., to north of Boston.

Here is a list of a few of the socioeconomic pressures that work to accelerate urban sprawl:

1) Overall increase in population;
2) Movement from the farms and outlying areas to the city;
3) Too high density in the inner city;
4) Decay of residences in the city core;
5) Rising economic means permits residents in the inner city to move to suburbs and residents in suburbs to move to larger homes on larger lots that are further out;
6) Development of extensive highway systems;

7)   The relocation of industry;

8)   Rising urban transportation problems.

These trends are, of course, interdependent, but once established, they seem to have a life of their own. Thus, possessing more than one car has become a family need beyond the family's actual need for basic transportation. Another example is the "self-perpetuating spiral" resulting from the policy of using gasoline taxes primarily for highway construction. This makes it feasible to build new highways and facilitate building new tracts of homes farther away from metropolitan centers. This, in turn, leads to greater use of cars and more gasoline taxes to construct more roads, more homes, and so on, in an ever increasing spiral spurred on by population and the other pressures listed above.

Let us now examine some of the consequences of *urban sprawl.* Later we will see how a total-system approach to urban planning might enhance some of the good features of urbanization and avoid some of the negative aspects.

Consequences of Urban Sprawl – Good and Bad

Granted that vast urban sprawls exist and will undoubtedly continue to spread unabated, so what? For many, a suburban home or apartment is a very comfortable place to be. To those who have recently escaped from the inner city the suburbs are wonderful places indeed! According to Alvin Toffler, author of the book *Future Shock,* "The working masses in the high-technology societies are totally indifferent to the call for a political revolution aimed at exchanging one form of property ownership for another.

For most people the rise in affluence has meant a better, not a worse, existence, and they look upon their much despised 'suburban middle-class lives' as fulfillment rather than deprivation."

But the "fulfillment" Toffler refers to is not free of inconveniences. Some of these inconveniences have come about so gradually that many people have grown to accept them. Take the daily commute. Portal to portal time (the total time a worker spends away from home for employment) varies. Based on an informal spot survey by the authors, moderate income professional workers in metropolitan areas spend around three hours a day (on the average) commuting. Typically for the larger cities, about an hour to an hour and a half of the principal wage earners' day is spent in portal-to-portal travel. Mothers spend a good part of each day chauffeuring their children because streets are unsafe, distances have become too far to walk, and public transportation is too infrequent or is nonexistent. The decision as to where to shop is often based on how convenient it is to drive to and to park. Many people do not want to shop (or go to a theater) downtown in big cities any more if it involves the use of an automobile. It's not worth the time and effort to fight the traffic and the parking is too inconvenient and too expensive.

Streets are dangerous places. In a metropolitan area with a population of two million there are over 500 traffic deaths and 6,000 injuries per year. Highway accidents have become just another abstract statistic. According to the National Highway Traffic Safety Administration, there approximately 100,000 car accidents that are due to 'drowsy driving' each year. It's estimated to result in 1,550 deaths, 71,000 injuries, and $12.5

billion in monetary losses. On quiet streets in the suburbs, much time and effort is spent organizing activities to keep small children from getting run over by cars. Often gardens and homes are fenced in for this reason. It is well to reflect on the psychological effect that all this shepherding and isolation must have on the growing child.

The relation of smog to urban sprawl is well known. The more sprawl there is, and the more the residential, commercial, recreational, and shopping functions are zoned apart from each other, the greater will be the energy expended in getting people and materials back and forth between them, and so the greater will be their contribution to air pollution. Everything is interrelated. The question is: What effect do population trends, patterns of urban growth, zoning, and improved exhaust devices or fuel, have on air quality? One thing is certain: if there is to be an improvement in air quality under the present governmental approach, it will have to come about by equipping factories with expensive antipollution devices, by further modifying the design of cars, by using smaller vehicles and different types of fuels, by curtailing the use of cars and by developing mass transit, and so on. All have a price tag and it means that direct and indirect costs of transportation will be even higher. The direct cost of transportation now runs about 10 percent of the budget of a moderate income family. Later, we will show that alternative designs for urban areas could make more effective use of time and space, that these would be economically feasible because of the resultant savings in transportation alone.

Most people seem to derive pleasure out of their ability to control an automobile and to drive cheaply and comfortably for long distances. To them, the automobile is nothing short of wonderful. It gives freedom to go where and when one chooses. With a car one can live in the most remote of areas. One can go for a ride with a girl-friend and park in privacy where there is a lovely view. If people are unhappy, it is not with the automobile per se but with the inconvenience and cost incurred when it needs repair, with the tension of driving on high-speed crowded freeways, with the bumper-to-bumper traffic jams, and with the problems of finding a parking place. Indeed we have become so enamored with the auto that we have gone to great lengths on its behalf. Lewis Mumford, the well-known social philosopher and authority on cities, describes the passion this way:

The current way of life is founded not just on motor transportation but on the religion of the motorcar, and the sacrifices that people are prepared to make for this religion stand outside the realm of rational criticism. Perhaps the only thing that could bring Americans to their senses would be a clear demonstration of the fact that their highway program will, eventually, wipe out the very area of freedom that the private motorcar promised to retain for them.

What Lewis Mumford laments are the patchwork planning that allows an auto-based transportation system to displace all other transportation forms. In his book *The Highway and the City* he tries to warn the British not to follow in American footsteps. He cites Oxford, England as an example of a city that has "suffered incredible devastation" from the overuse of the automobile. Mumford predicts that soon the entire British Isles will become a greater Oxford, with an ever increasing number of car owners vainly seeking to escape, at a high speed that turns into a crawl, into a countryside that no longer exists. Cities, in turn, will be transformed into extravagant parking lots; and before you awaken from this nightmare you may, if you ignore the experience of Los Angeles, Detroit, Boston, and hundred other American centers, dismantle the one kind of transportation that would, if properly organized, rescue you from this fate: the railroad.

Morris Neiburger, an expert on air pollution, states it a little differently:

"I don't believe controls can be devised that will adequately reduce the poisons given off by automobiles and other machines that burn fossil fuels (such as gas and oil). All civilization will pass away, not from a sudden cataclysm like a nuclear war, but from gradual suffocation in its own wastes."

The consequence of this uncontrolled use of the automobile in a rapidly growing urban area leads eventually to an impossible transportation problem at the urban center. One after-the-damage-is-done solution is mass transit. Many planners feel that the best way to eliminate chaotic transportation habits within cities is to construct satellite cities, in which people can live in a satellite community that is close to the part of the city in which they work. Others feel that the answer lies in rebuilding the inner city, using superblock apartments, each superblock surrounded by green space, with good transportation from these to the city center. We will discuss these and other planning solutions later.

The central city has suffered from the flight of its citizens to suburbia. With their departure went their tax money and their interest in civic affairs. As the vitality of the city was sapped, slum conditions were aggravated. But there are other consequences. The replacement of a slum with a superblock project looks beautiful on paper. In practice, these projects have profoundly altered the structure of community life and not always for the better. For example, street life, which some planners consider "unwholesome" and which disappears when superblocks are built, has, in its hustle and bustle and unstructured supervision, a positive component in raising raise kids successfully, according to Jane Jacobs. Community life in the suburbs has also been found wanting. The practice of fencing in homes and gardens (for privacy and protection) and the practices of using the car for every errand have the effect of isolating the family from personal encounters with those who live in the neighborhood. To address this we run the risk of becoming overly friendly with one's next door neighbors and losing one's privacy. Apparently there is no happy in-between and so one usually ends up staying isolated. Again this raises questions: Is this a good environment to be in? Is it really secure against crime? Is it good for raising children?

Concerns about pollution, about the preservation of wildlife, about man's effect on the ecosystem, and about the kind of world left for future generations have become national issues. Most people feel that something must be done to undo man's negative impact on nature, but the accelerative thrust of fast-moving world societies has left everyone with a feeling of utter helplessness. The key question is always: If we stop the "progress" that harms the environment in one place, do we only make it worse somewhere else?

Clearly, many of the problems connected with urban sprawl could be avoided by *total-system-planning*. The problems of urban development are too crucial to the future to be left to real estate developers and urban planning authorities who recommend more freeways, multilevel parking facilities, and other patchwork cures.

The *total-system approach* is a term that refers to methods for evaluating the effects of a proposed design on as many aspects of the urban system as possible – in particular, operations research, mathematical models, and computers can all be used to simulate and analyze the total system. We discuss details of this in Part Two. As the observant reader will soon note that while we point out the need for a total-system approach, there are many aspects of the city, such as the form of its government its economic and educational systems, or the way it handles race relations, that we can only touch upon. These are important areas that should be studied in the context of a compact city. However, in the interest of keeping the book short, we have placed the emphasis on those aspects which, in our opinion, would be substantially affected by our proposal to make more effective use of space and time, the vertical and time dimensions.

PROTECTION FROM THREATS TO HUMAN SURVIVAL

There are numerous reasons why people and countries have to consider Compact cities seriously. Both the size of the world population and the environment are changing dynamically to a point where we have to consider the challenges and threats they pose. The future is not going to be a simple perturbation of the present. Not for long. It has become essential to minimize or eliminate traffic problems, energy conservation, social integration and even to preserve civilization and progress as we know them now. With the rapidly increasing population and world integration, as it has been with the economic sector, a revolutionary rather than an evolutionary outcome for city design is needed.

Along with a compact city design there should also be a compact agricultural design that protects farms from calamities, a subject for another book. It could save human civilization in case of extreme natural disasters, like the eruption in April 1815 of the volcano Tambora located on Sumbawa Island in the southern chain of the Indonesian archipelago, the largest volcanic eruption in recorded history that locally killed more than 71,000 people but also created global climate anomalies that led to the disastrous "volcanic winter" in 1816, the so-called "Year Without a Summer" because of the effect on European and North American weather. Agricultural crops failed and livestock died in much of the Northern Hemisphere, resulting in the worst famine of the 19th century.

In the Toba catastrophe theory of 70 to 75 thousand years ago, a super volcanic event at Lake Toba in Sumatra, Indonesia, reduced the human population of the world to an estimated 10,000 or even 1,000 breeding pairs, creating a bottleneck in human evolution. It also killed three quarters of all plant life in the northern hemisphere.

Then there was the six-mile-wide asteroid Chicxulub which slammed into the Earth more than 65 million years ago in the Yucatán Peninsula in Mexico where there is now a village by that name. It is linked to a major biological catastrophe in which more than 50 percent of the Earth's species, including the dinosaurs, became extinct.

The Huang He (Yellow River) in China floods particularly often. The Great Flood of 1931 caused between 800,000 and 4,000,000 deaths. The 1998 Yangtze River Floods, in China, left 14 million people homeless. In 2005, an Indian Ocean tsunami, triggered by a magnitude 9.0 earthquake, killed 230,000 in a dozen countries. On March 11, 2011, a magnitude-9.0 earthquake and tsunami devastated a long stretch of Japan's northeastern coast, killed about 19,000 people, and put a giant crimp in Japan's production of electricity using nuclear power.

The following all pose a threat to the lives of lots of people. Earthquakes, blizzards, cyclonic storms, hurricanes, tsunamis, tornadoes, droughts, famines, epidemics, solar flares, gamma ray bursts, floods, fires and radiation contamination and even the melting of the southern polar ice cap with its two mile high, five million square mile ice whose total melting over time could cause the rise of sea water to cover lands to more than 200 feet, and most great cities in the world today would be submerged. La Paz and Quito are small and are examples of exceptions because of their high altitudes. Hurricanes and tornadoes are known to cause a lot of damage in the United States. Much loss of life and property are known to happen because of the lack of protection of the environment particularly to hurricane force winds.

We are at a point in our development when we can build cities that are sufficiently planned and designed to protect human civilization. Security is becoming increasingly critical to the functioning of our daily tasks.   Cities themselves, our industries, and our technology are the biggest drivers motivating us to build safer cities. The threat to the security of our cities means we will depend more and more on local authorities and local law enforcement services. The need for security on so many fronts in our modern complex world has changed the role of the city to assuming social responsibility and looking out for the well-being of its citizens.

A completely covered compact city constructed on the side of a mountain and near a river or a lake can help protect its inhabitants from flooding, volcanic eruptions that darken the earth for a long time, from tsunamis and other natural disasters including large meteors that hit the earth and bring about the extinction of life on earth. Because the light from the sun may be blocked by gases in the atmosphere for a long time the city will need compact forms of nuclear energy because it may be very difficult or hazardous to move fuels over long distances. The city will have to grow its own food in green houses using its nuclear derived electric energy. To assure the survival of mankind we can build such self-contained compact cities in many different places on earth to assure that some will survive any natural disaster.

OUR OBJECTIVES

It seems to us that there are a number of reasonable goals that constitute a better quality of life. Primarily, urban areas should be designed to provide these things:

1) A good life but not at the expense of future generations
2) A viable center for business, culture, sports, and government
3) A new start for the disadvantaged

Urban areas should also provide:

1) Ample sized living spaces

2) Private gardens (for those who desire them)
3) Work and shopping within walking distance from home
4) Clean air, water, and a pollution-free environment
5) Easy access to natural recreation areas, and to top cultural and shopping centers
6) Major activity centers that are close to each other
7) Freedom from frustrating delays
8) A safe environment for children
9) Low density
10) Flexibility

James W. Rouse, the architect who designed Columbia, Maryland, expresses his goals for new towns a little differently:

1) The elimination of all slum and blight.
2) A job for everyone who needs work or wants work.
3) Good housing for everyone at rents and prices he can afford.
4) Education designed to meet the people – youth and adults – at their point of need, and to help them grow as individuals.
5) Health facilities to build health prevent illness; provide best possible care at lowest possible cost.
6) Recreation facilities close to home, appropriate to the various age groups, from tiny kids to old people.
7) A police system that works scientifically and resourcefully to rid the city of organized crime and works humanely and sympathetically at the neighborhood level to develop respect for law and order and assist the deviant to learn and grow.
8) A communication system that makes it easy for people to know about one another, to be informed about life and activity in their neighborhood as well as in the larger community.

9) A transportation system that allows people to move easily, pleasantly, and inexpensively throughout the city without dependence upon private automobiles.

10) Parks, playgrounds, green areas threading through the city to bring nature, beauty, repose, and space close to all people; also, to assist in breaking up the city into neighborhoods that will be in a scale with people; capable of being identified, embraced, managed by the people who live here.

11) Arrangement of housing, schools, churches, stores, health and recreation facilities, in such relationship to one another within a neighborhood that people will have easy, natural opportunity to one another and their teachers, ministers, merchants, doctors, public officials; share joys, sorrows, and common problems; reshape systems and institutions that don't work properly; build new ones to provide answers to their needs and yearnings; know that they have the opportunity to influence their destiny.

Note: he did not plan for cemeteries, they were added much later.

We could have chosen to discuss many possible designs simultaneously for new cities and to compare them with each other and to more conventional cities. We believe that such an approach would yield at best a blurred image of the various possibilities. Our hope is that by focusing on one possible new city, it will become more real in your imagination. If it should turn out to be not entirely to your taste, at the least it can serve as a base for thinking about your own most desired urban change.

The Compact City we will endeavor to explore with you would be economically inexpensive to build and maintain, yet spacious; it should have private gardens for those who want them, and public parks. Only a few minutes of travel time would separate homes from schools or work, and residents would be able to choose to walk, bicycle, or ride public transit. We will consider the advantages of having stores, restaurants, delivery service, health facilities, and all other routine services fully available, without delay, day or night, Monday or Sunday, winter or summer. In the Compact City we wish to establish there would, of course, be no urban sprawl, freeways, traffic, smog, or other forms of urban blight. The amount of land construction could be made flexible so that it would be easy to remodel, renew, and rearrange parts of the city, and thus avoid the process of urban decay that eventually results in slums.

Thinking of time as a dimension, we believe that Compact City would be the well-planned four-dimensional counterpart of our present-day predominantly two-dimensional cities, which are constantly being partially patched up to solve urban problems. The third dimension accounts for building upwards and the fourth dimension is time which allows the city to stay awake and alive on a 24 hour basis. The downtowns of large cities today are gradually utilizing more and more of the vertical dimension as buildings are torn down to be replaced by ever taller skyscrapers. The difference between today's cities and what we hope will characterize future cities is that expansion into full use of the vertical dimension today through the technique of tearing down and rebuilding results in cities that are many times more expensive, more inefficient and inflexible. Its buildings are not in full use nocturnally and are less attractive, and less exciting than Compact City because of their architectural limitations.

Ordinarily, man seeks change on a gradual basis. It would seem desirable to plan for such gradual change, but things are happening too fast. Past decisions are having negative effects at an accelerated rate. Society invests in freeways, a self-perpetuating mistake. As we have already seen, these invite greater urban sprawl, pollution, destruction of the countryside, and appalling death on the highways. They create a suburbia that has the unfortunate side effects of draining the money and the richness of life from the inner city. Suburbia, in turn, fosters long-distance travel to work, with corresponding waste of time commuting. And this creates the need for more and more extensive and expansive mass transit systems. The traditional patchwork approach of repairing and expanding present-day cities can only aggravate these trends, for they do not alleviate the pressures of an increasing population, rising expectations, inner-city decay, and industrial movement.

The objective then is to design a city that can grow, yet remain a convenient, simple, and exciting place to live. If possible we wish to design a city that preserves and enhances the good aspects of modern living, yet alleviates the population crisis, postpones the deterioration of the environment, and conserves the environment for the day when measures designed to control population become a reality. We will show that much can be done to improve cities. Compact City, as presented here, could be used as a yardstick of what might be expected if the patchwork approach is replaced by the total-system approach. What we think is remarkable is that Compact City, with all its spacious accommodations and accessibility, could be built largely by saving the cost of what is now wasted on transportation. In brief, Compact City should be a model city that demonstrates the feasibility of constructing new cities which would meet our needs and could be financed realistically.

CHALLENGES

The city is the gathering place where man creates and competes, works and plays. It is the web, the matrix that interlocks man with his fellow man. Modern man and his city are inseparable. His successes and failures take shape within its arena. It provides the source of motivation for those who wish to achieve. In the city man has been able to maintain a modicum of individuality and still be a member of a group with which he communicates and works. It is the citadel of stability and continuity for social institutions. But the city is also the stage for political unrest when the social and economic institutions fail to catch up with the rapid pace of changes in population and scientific progress, or when they fail to respond to the aspirations of its people.

All of society appears to be in an ever increasing state of flux. People change jobs more and more often. They are constantly moving from one home or apartment to another. Marriage partners are permuted and children of fractured families are redistributed. Businesses start up, shut down, expand, contract, and relocate. Schools consolidate and children are bussed to classes. Life becomes a game of "musical chairs."

The first challenge is to find a way of constructing the city so that it serves as a "platform" for flexibly changing and rearranging internal structures. Our current cities do not have the flexibility to meet the needs of a fast, turbulent, growing, trans-industrial society. The downtowns of cities try to adapt. They are an off mix of the new and the ancient – they are forever in a state of demolition, jack-hammering, and rebuilding. Unfortunately, once a building goes up, economics dictates that it remains until it rots. If the industrial or commercial area where we work is no longer suitable, the city's inflexible construction usually forces a major uprooting. If the decision is to relocate, the move leaves behind those who could not or would not adapt. A change to a new job in another part of town means enduring a frustrating commute, or else uprooting the family and forcing its members to find new neighbors, friends, teachers, and places to shop.

The second challenge concerns political organization. Present city administration is faced with a dilemma. It must create opportunity for its poor and renew its deteriorating areas with programs which require tax money. But city politicians no longer have the backing of wealthy communities that identify with the city's hopes and aspirations. The city has its poor, it has its commuters who often do not pay taxes, and it has businesses which are only too ready to move. Essentially, the problem becomes one of political jurisdiction, for the technical and financial means to revitalize city life exist in the combined city and its surrounding sprawl, i.e., in the megalopolis as a whole. The challenge is to restructure the design of the city so that the exploding pressures that drove families to the suburbs will become an implosion bringing them back to the city.

The third challenge has to do with conservation. The encroachment of creeping suburbia on the countryside has destroyed valuable farm land that may be needed one day to provide food to meet the population crisis. It has destroyed the ability of urban man to have easy access to unspoiled nature; this is, in effect, a kind of destruction of man's soul. More important, vast ecological problems have been created that can only be alleviated by the effective redesign of the city to conserve land, water, energy, and waste. Cities consume enormous quantities of water, electricity, and petroleum and other fuels, but reprocess little of their waste products. A major technological challenge is to redesign the city in such a way as to make it possible to share facilities, to conserve resources, and to contribute positively to the environment and to the future.

In the end the challenges merge and become one with our objectives – namely, try to make our cities into convenient, simple, exciting places to live; to make them more flexible to changing needs, more compact in order to curtail sprawl, and to be less destructive of the natural environment, with the hope that population growth will be curbed before the countryside disappears.

Our technological society is able and well equipped to prepare a better world for all our children and children of our children; and yet, only the most meager of technical ideas are pursued for the benefit of the billions who will live in tomorrow's cities. Instead, material resources and energy are dissipated negatively in the pursuit of nationalism, war, and power.

In the chapters that follow we shall try to outline an approach, which we shall call the total-system interactive approach, for redesigning cities. But first let us see how some of the well-known contributors to urban development view the problems we have just outlined, and let us take a look at some of their proposed solutions.

A CHALLENGING EXERCISE: WHAT KIND OF COMPACT CITY TO BUILD?

The future city project challenge is to delve into the details of various future city models and aims at finding which model design would be most suitable for a particular city, given its unique situation and condition.   For example, although a round shape seems to be frequently proposed, we need to evaluate other shapes as well. Other issues to consider could include:

- The size or detailed design needs to accommodate the current, expected, or even the maximum number of people, in the city, who either live there or simply work there or go there on a daily basis, traveling from their homes in the suburbs or outside the city. Here the types of buildings/utilization (offices, garden/plants, stores, schools, hospitals/clinics, apartments, houses, parking lot, open space outside/inside) would be an issue to address, as well as the location of different types of buildings for optimum distance from private to public places.

- The number of levels would need to be determined carefully for preventing excessive pressure at the base and other unusual tall building problems, including efficient spacing between levels for the feeling of openness but not at very high cost. Here there is an issue of structural support design (pressure at the base, spacing of vertical columns), level of rigidity or alterability of the different parts of the construction, as well as the means to move vertically between levels (ramps, escalators, stairs, elevators). A home delivery system would be an issue that might be unique in very tall buildings.

- The transportation system outside/inside the city will pose its challenge as well.

CIRCULAR COMPACT CITIES

The idea behind the compact circular city is to take advantage of circular design where all points at the circumference are equidistant from the center. The central part of a circular city will be mainly reserved for residential colonies. The preferred housing type is apartment dwellings and community housing where a lot of people can stay together. Housing being at the center would ensure better security for the residents as none of the homes will be left aloof for any potential danger. Staying in close vicinity will also ensure very good social relations and a sense of trust and security.

The rest of the infrastructure would be constructed around the center in various shells. The need for a particular product or service determines its relative location from the center. For example, a major retail store can be located on the first shell or ground floor, around the center, as it enjoys maximum proximity to everyone and caters to the most frequent needs. Schools can be located at the second level and hospitals at the third level. The outermost level should be reserved for industrial setups. There are multiple benefits of having the industrial setup at the periphery such as the industrial pollution in the form of toxic gases will stay far from the residential areas and thus would ensure better health. Industrial traffic would not enter into the city causing less city congestion.

Another benefit of having a circular compact city is the ease of designing an efficient public transport system where the public transport vehicles would service from central housing to the periphery in all direction and across various shells.

The circular city has the limitation that once the design of the city is finalized there is very little scope for further expansion. A network of compact circular cities close to one another is one way to resolve the expansion problem.

Once the circular city is designed it would solve the problems pertaining to public transport as most places would be equidistant from the residential area and more people would be using the public transport. Thus a network of compact circular cities would help in resolving problems related to congestion within the cities and ensure better living standards for all.

ELEVATED CITY

An elevated city is designed to prevent the uncontrolled plundering of the natural landscape by developers and industry.

At current rates the surface of the planet will be nearly totally covered with residential, commercial and apartment dwellings within the coming two centuries. Large structures bring nature upward to preserve the natural surroundings and also to add natural surroundings in a controlled environment.

In the elevated city the upper level wall thicknesses are the same as those of the lower level ones, unlike other structural systems that are extremely tall. The scale of this structure would be such that an entire large city of today should fit into its base. One must not think in terms of floors but, instead, imagine entire landscaped neighborhood districts with "skies" that are 30 to 50 meters high.

Figure 3-3 Picture of elevated city (probably from a science fiction movie by Barreto Multimedia)

Lakes, streams, rivers, hills and ravines comprise the soil landscape on which residential, office, commercial, retail and entertainment buildings can be built. The concept can be thought of as what would happen if nature grew upwards with multi-soil levels. The buildings structure can be thought of as a giant stainless steel net stretched and anchored over a central high-strength concrete hollow core with a double helix configuration. The exterior walls are made of structural glass that conforms to the crisscrossing, double helix, cable strand tension system that disperses all exterior forces along the surface. If wind or earthquake shock waves push or disturb one portion of the structure the other portion absorbs and dissipates the forces.

Ecological efficiency is a rule and all areas of the structure feature resource conserving technology such as recycled building materials, compost toilets, nature-based water cleansing systems for all buildings, plentiful amounts of forest, plant life and water-based ecosystems.

In essence, elevated city is more an ecosystems design than an architectural habitation design. The structure provides a basis for architectural development upon which architectural diversity can flourish. Sunlight is brought into the center of the structure by means of a hollow, mirrored core that reflects sunlight and disperses it within the structure. This allows for both interior and exterior sunlight to exist in plentiful amounts. The tower sits in a natural setting in a large lake. Lake water is drawn up throughout the structure and used for cooling floors and walls. A portion of this water is heated by large passive solar panels and left to fall by gravity to be used at the various levels. No internal combustion engines or toxic pollutants exist within the confines of the structure. Everything will be managed by hydrogen gas, electrical or water powered and all heating cooling is regulated by plants and trees.

The natural beauty of nature is preserved by condensing the areas of living, working environments, commerce and industry into an upwardly directed architectural structure.

Figure 3-4 (Source: http://cdn.home-designing.com/wp-content/uploads/2008/11/56.jpg)

Multi-storied gardens are to be infused with architectural components. The presence of natural sunlight, fresh air, breeze and panoramic views are to be of primary importance. Ease and quickness of transportation vertically and laterally is crucial. The building will be fireproof, waterproof, can resist great wind velocities and is very earthquake resistant.

An example of the trumpet bell shape, modeled after the highest structure created by a creature other than human, the termite's nest structures of Africa (Figure 3-5), is a most efficient form for their compressive characteristics allowing the thickness of the upper supporting walls to be uniform in thickness down through the bottom of the building. No other shape can dispel loads from top to bottom, is effectively aerodynamic and retains such stability in a tall building. Inside is a complex design that has been studied and copied by humans. Internal mound temperatures remain a constant 87 degrees F, according to AskNature.org, despite outside temperatures in the range of 35 to 104 degrees F. The termites incorporate a system of vents at the top and bottom of the mound to allow cool air to come in through the bottom and warm air to escape through the top.

Figure 3-5 A termite nest (or city?)

Cooling is based on the African termite nest model where the bottom spaces are cooled with water, in this case waterfalls, where cool air builds up and replaces warm air and is warmed by bodily activity in the upper floors and exits through different levels of the building. Simultaneously all floors have specially designed windows with aerodynamic wind cowls, so that windows can be opened without having to resist tremendous wind forces. These cowls direct air throughout the interior spaces by acting as natural air-conditioners.

In the elevated or trumpet bell city, large bodies of water are placed at separate levels and serve multiple functions; as fire barriers and fire sprinkler system reservoirs, as recycled water catch basins, as recreational lakes, rivers, waterfalls and streams. Wherever possible, whole ecosystems are supported within the building.

Transportation in the city will be mass transportation systems which run on natural energy generated from solar energy.

Figure 3-6 Pleasant water spaces abound inside

Figure 3-7 Skyscraper garden (source: Tokyo skyscraper garden
http://hydroponicaccess.com/wp-
content/uploads/2010/10/garden3.jpg)

A series of reflecting mirrors bring direct sunlight into the interior
of the building, so that yards and garden areas are exposed to the
sun without the danger of high wind velocities. The immense
surface area of the building, sheathed with photovoltaic solar
cells, provides most of the electrical energy requirements. All
spaces would have a healthy feeling of cross-circulation and
higher floors would have thinner air than the lower floors–just as
it is naturally. Persons who wish to work and live in a higher sea
level environment can now do so within the building.

GREEN HOUSE CITY

The idea of this city is to use natural forms and resources to build
future houses and cities. Generally the material like cement,

concrete and other things used to build tall buildings are not environment friendly and create pollution. Concrete buildings absorb a lot of heat from the atmosphere which makes the interiors of the building hot. In many cities trees are being cut to make space for high rise buildings, reducing green cover. The global warming phenomenon is another major side effect of the reduction in green cover.

The idea of a Green House City is to build houses in the trunks of trees or on trees. The house will be designed so that the entire structure, furniture and other accessories are made up of tree parts. The houses will be coated from inside and outside with a special substance that prevents the trees from rotting and breaking down. All the furniture will be made from wood and leaves. All utensils will be from fine teak wood which is durable and can be cleaned very easily. Transportation in the city will be by vehicles powered by bio-fuels and people will be encouraged to use public transportation. Carpooling will be made compulsory and the public will receive incentives to use it. The city will burn landfill methane gas to power electric generators and as electricity produced from landfill methane is considered green power, it can be used extensively. Such methane use will also earn credits in various programs designed to limit carbon emissions and decrease the use of fossil fuels. The city will also try using city buses running on renewable power such as: hybrid power supplies which combine solar panels, suspension-piezo-power, and super-air-ion cells.

Figure 3-8 (Source: http://cdn.home-designing.com/wp-content/uploads/2008/11/18.jpg)

The use of natural resources such as coal, oil and gas will be minimal and restricted. All industries will be at a certain distance from the residential colonies and would be surrounded by carefully designed tree cover to absorb all the harmful gases emitted. The city will be sustainable and self-sufficient. All food requirements will be satisfied inside the city itself. Technology will be used to protect the houses from natural calamities.

While there are some advantages to the green house concept, there are many challenges as well. First, this concept cannot be implemented in countries and regions where the climate is not favorable and the trees need to retain the cover all the time. Not all trees have a long enough life to sustain a normal house. The tree house may not be able to provide all the comforts and luxuries in a high rise apartment. There will also be challenges on a community and social level. Even if the houses are cost effective to build, getting people to accept the drastic change from a brick shelter to a natural tree house will be a real problem.

With all the challenges expected to be encountered, and weighing it against the benefits which can possibly be accrued, Green House City is a good possible design for a future city.

WATER CITY

Water cities will consist of a system of structures that can easily accommodate many millions of people and relieve the land based population pressures. They can provide the inhabitants with information and serve as natural sea aquariums without artificially enclosing marine life.

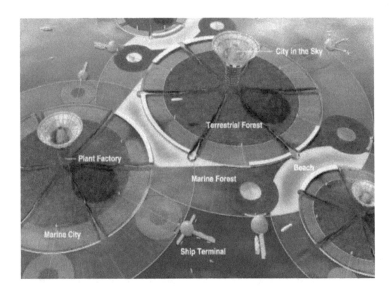

Figure 3-9 The Botanical City Concept (Shimizu Corporation)
http://www.shimz.co.jp/english/theme/dream/greenfloat.html

Shimizu Corporation writes of its botanical city: "After construction, these structures can be towed to various locations where they would be most beneficial, then anchored to the ocean floor. Some structures will be towed in prefabricated segments and then joined together at selected locations. Their internal construction will include floatation chambers which will render them practically unsinkable. They can be self-maintained and fully automated."

Shimizu Corporation also writes: "Offshore apartment buildings of concrete, steel, glass, titanium, and a wide variety of new synthetic materials could be built to relieve the population pressure. The materials used in such projects will be engineered to withstand the corrosive effects of the harsh ocean environment." The examples shown below of other water cities are from Jacque Fresco's Venus Project.

Figure 3-10 The Venus Project (Jacque Fresco) from
http://www.thevenusproject.com/

Figure 3-11 The Venus Project (Jacque Fresco)
http://www.thevenusproject.com/

Figure 3-12 The Venus Project (Jacque Fresco)
http://www.thevenusproject.com/

Other ocean cities will maintain sea farms that will cultivate many forms of marine life. They could also be used as a new resource for mining the relatively untapped resources of the oceans without disturbing its ecology.

Figure 3-13 Watercity in Dubai, "lilypad floating city" from:
http://www.being-here.net/page/5143/en

Still others may monitor and maintain environmental equilibrium and reclaim dangerous radioactive and other pollutant materials that have been dumped into the sea. This is a concept of a marine culture and sea-farming system, which will be used to cultivate and raise fish and other forms of marine life to help meet the nutritional needs of the world's people. Palm Island, located in the sea off Dubai, is an example of such construction.

INFORMATION MANAGEMENT AND METHODS

Spatial information has become indispensable for many aspects of urban development, planning and management. The increasing importance of spatial information has been due to recent progress in spatial information (especially satellite remote sensing and positioning), management (using geographic information systems and database tools) and access (witnessing the growth in web mapping services) as well as the development of analytical techniques such as high resolution mapping of urban environments. These more efficient techniques can lead to a wider diversity as well as more up to date information.

On the one hand, planners and implementers of intersectoral interventions need to appreciate the unique challenges their approach poses to the conducting of evaluations. On the other hand, evaluators need to grasp the contextual influences on implementation if they are to design valid, implementable and policy-relevant evaluation studies. Successful evaluation requires practitioners and evaluators to find a common language so they can collaborate.

The greatest challenge for evaluators is complexity, which is multi-dimensional, influencing more than one outcome, and operating in sometimes hard to describe environments. Intersectoral interventions present complexity on every aspect of development. Thus an evaluator's first task would be to understand the contextual variables that influence cities and intersectoral interventions. It becomes a prerequisite for solving the more familiar tasks of choosing outcomes, designing evaluation studies, collecting data and interpreting findings. Evaluators also need to understand the dynamic spatial characteristics of the settings in which they work, as well as to appreciate the temporal changes in the types of interventions they evaluate.

The IBM Institute for Business Value proposes basic steps to help city leaders begin to make improvements, especially in times of extreme financial constraints:

1) Decide what your city should be – determine its brand (identify and work on differentiating strengths that will attract skills, knowledge, and creativity);

2) Adopt policies conducive to skills, creativity, and knowledge driven growth (attract internationally mobile talent, create a domestic talent base, retain the existing base of talent);

3) Optimize around the citizen (begin tailored services, create linkage across city core systems, develop a clear and transparent system of user fees and charges)

4) Employ systems thinking in all aspects of planning and management;

5) Develop and apply information technologies to improve core city systems.

Chapter 4

Compact City Structure

An Essay

Recent authors and urban planners have appropriated the term Compact City to advocate a dense urban development plan that seeks to eliminate urban sprawl and emphasize sustainability. Originally, it referred to a rather different approach to urban planning — one structurally and programmatically unlike any currently proposed project or existing city. Of course, architecture and urban planning, intertwined inextricably with society on all levels, have been notoriously slow to pick up new ideas in those fields less constrained by fiscal, social, political and other concerns. Hence, we present Compact City in its original form, with some new suggestions in the hope that others might take the plan as a jumping off point to draw their own conclusions about what our environment could and perhaps should be like.

Compact City is a proposal seeking to develop a sense of community that can survive the tumultuous Twenty-First Century. With more than half of the world now living in urban areas, its proposal offers potential solutions to increasingly pressing issues regarding the way in which we all live and interact. Whether it is used as a platform for new and quite possibly better solutions or direct application in city design, we hope that it may act as a catalyst for change regarding our overall understanding of what it means to be city builders as well as city dwellers.

While one dream lives on, another one dies. The dream of a utopia is usually about a place where people live quietly and closely, where automobiles are rarely seen and heard. That dream started dying a long time ago. Except for a few dedicated efforts to preserve the utopia, there are few places in the world the car has not touched.

Much of this chapter on structure is borrowed from the 1973 edition of Compact City, written by Dantzig and Saaty, and is meant primarily to summarize the structure and organization of the city as presented in that book. Earlier, we explored the social consequences of new solutions that implement technology that has emerged since the publication of the first book. But here, we summarize the proposed structure of Compact City.

Because of the lack of forethought when building our cities, we are now off on the wrong foot. Greater urban sprawl, pollution, destruction of the countryside, and appalling death on the highways are all sub-optimal outcomes of an ad hoc planning process. The approach creates a suburbia that has the unfortunate side effects of draining the money and the richness of life from the inner city. Suburbia, in turn, fosters long-distance travel to work, with corresponding time lost in commuting. And this creates the need for more and more extensive and expansive mass transit systems.

Many may balk at the audacity of two mathematicians attempting such a sweeping retreatment of urban planning. But the authors are explicit in their belief that change can and should happen. According to their research in 1973, they suggest that the means exist to meet these challenges. Our technological society is well equipped to prepare a better world for all our children and generations to come; and yet, only the most meager of technical ideas are pursued for the benefit of the billions who will live in tomorrow's cities. Instead, material resources and energy are dissipated negatively in the pursuit of nationalism, war, and power. A number of architects, urban planners, and scholars in general have said the same, though their approaches are varied and often contradictory.

Dantzig and Saaty in their original Compact City book considered many ideas for future cities—from Charles-Édouard Le Corbusier's Radiant City to Jane Jacobs' scathing critique of modern planning. As they say, we appreciate the inherent and salutary diversity in human nature. Different people want different things and prefer to live where there is a choice of environmental settings. We believe there would be a framework for greater diversity in Compact City. This is a city that hopes to establish itself as an open platform for thinking about future cities, as well as a basic model for construction that could, given analytic blueprints and investment, be implemented in the very near future.

These methods have been self-described as the total-system interactive approach, a succinct rendering of the objectives as stated above. Thus this book as well as its predecessor, attempts to delineate many aspects of this imagined city as possible, in an effort to grasp the complex interactions of space, time, individual and society. But what are we designing for? The goals we might wish to achieve in a well-designed city might include:

1) An aesthetic environment
2) As many labor-saving conveniences as possible
3) Rapid access to any part of the city

4) A suitable climate
5) Low-cost living
6) Conservation of agricultural land
7) Easy access to natural surroundings
8) Elimination of delays
9) Reduced pollution
10) The elimination of auto accidents
11) The prevention of sabotage
12) The minimization of the possibility of being trapped in the city in case of a disaster.

The final plan must somehow reconcile these multiple goals. The plan must make clear how much of one goal would have to be sacrificed to attain more of another. Presented in this form it is possible for the citizens or their designated representatives to make intelligent decisions as to whether or not to accept a plan or to request modification of it.

Thus compact city becomes a model for further development. The idea of a model is to express relationships, some of which we can control or change, and some of which are as immutable as a law of physics. The model is the framework which allows us to consider the alternatives and select the "best" plan. Thus the term "model" as used here means a "model generator," i.e., a way to generate many particular "model realizations" for comparison and selection.

Modeling a total system is a serious art, the systematic assembly of an enormous amount of information in a form that is tractable for prediction and intelligent action. There is no such thing as *the* model for the economic life of a region, or for a city within that region; nor is there a single total framework to serve for modeling the world.

Ultimately, the authors suggest, we have little choice but to develop such total-system models and solutions. Piecemeal corrections will hardly suffice to restore an environment shaped by long term abuse. Even in 1973 the authors understood that man treats his environment selfishly, stripping away what he wants and dumping what he doesn't, actions taken in the name of "economics." Indeed, in planning, the future is discounted so heavily that only the immediate present (for example, the next five years) has any value. About the only thing we hesitate to do is to remove our ancestors from their graves to make room for highways and housing.

But now we are faced with investing larger efforts to restore and preserve processes of nature which may in the future determine whether or not man survives. Often, trying to make amends for man's environmental destruction becomes a vicious cycle. Eliminate air pollution and you create water pollution. Build a treatment plant for the fouled water and you've got solid waste to dispose of. The environment is complex. There appear to be no easy solutions to problems of environmental abuse; their resolutions require gathering the knowledge from many fields and using good planning techniques to make the most effective use of this knowledge. Hence, we have placed so much emphasis on modeling the total system through making use of operations research and computers.

To demonstrate the total system approach as developed in Compact City, let us review what the city could potentially look like. We will begin from the outside, and work our way inside, exploring the multiple systems and spaces within the cities basic layout. To begin:

One would see no tall buildings – only a landscaped plateau park raised 240 feet above the surrounding countryside. Into the tiered slopes forming the edges of this plateau would be built apartments, patios, and roads. These exterior roads would permit one to ascend (in a quarter turn about the perimeter) to the plateau atop the city. Inside, in the interior of the city, more apartments, homes, offices, and work centers are relocated on several levels.

The plateau on top of the city gives a panorama of rural countryside. Immediately beyond the city would be recreational areas, all within ten minutes by car or bus from any part of the city. (The Park-Roof and the surrounding environs of the city constitute 100 square miles of recreational areas immediately available to all inhabitants). Also visible from the city top is the airport. Underground all-weather roads connect the airport to the city. Railroad freight cars are marshaled beyond the airport and enter the city when they can be immediately unloaded or reloaded. Heavy industries, such as power plants and oil refineries are located in an industrial park just beyond the airport, in the proximity of the railroad yards. All other industry is inside the city.

As Moshe Safdie, designer of the Montreal Habitat, writes: "We want two extremes. We want the intensive meeting place, the urban environment, the place where everybody is together, and we want the secluded open space where we are alone in the country with nature. We need and want both...This is the contradictory desire in our utopia...We want to live in a small community with which we can identify and yet we want all the facilities of the city of millions of people. We want to have very intense urban experiences and yet we want the open space right next to us."

Compact City attempts to resolve this problem in a rather unique fashion. It very blatantly would give residents both extremes. Rather than a suburban home, which offers a diluted experience of both "urbanity" and "nature" (neither truly available), Compact City literally combines a remarkably dense urban space with nature and countryside in their most uncongested form. The city itself, then, resides *within* this vast superstructure—a bizarre proposal, with remarkable implications.

What then, is this structure itself like? According to Dantzig and Saaty:

Physically, Compact City can be thought of as a three-dimensional organic structure designed for convenient living for its inhabitants during the various stages of its development. The essential idea is that the city *builds* its own "land" instead of robbing nature. Various-sized lots would be made available on different levels; on these lots one could build offices, plants, stores, schools, apartments, and houses very much like one would in a conventional city (except that in Compact City a more flexible construction could be used since the facilities are protected from weather). On the lots one could build homes in various styles and the remaining open space could be used for patios and interior gardens.

The city grows by increasing by the size of its base and the number of its levels. If it were to grow to a maximum size of

2,000,000 people, it would have a base of nine square miles and 16 levels. The same city, if laid out flat on the earth's surface, would cover an area of 140 square miles.

Compact City's maximum height would be about that of a conventional 36-story building. Note, however that Compact City would exert less pressure at the base because it would have only 16 levels widely separated in height instead of 36 narrowly cramped together. Hence, as far as height or weight is concerned, the construction of the city should not cause any unusual building problems. The 256 or so main elevators (spaced about 1,000 feet apart along radials in the city) use a negligible area. The system of ramps within the city makes it easy for trucks to bring materials *to any level* during construction. What this means is that it should be no more costly to construct the higher levels of Compact City (per square foot) than to construct a low one-or two-story building.

Structurally, the support design for Compact City may be likened to that of a typical high-rise apartment building. However, because of the large interior open areas it can also be likened to the support design of a multilevel car-park facility. The proposed spacing between levels of 30 feet or more was made part of the design in order to contribute to the feeling of openness. Because of the large open volumes the average weight per square foot on the foundations would be less than 1/3 of that for the same height found in conventional structures. The spacing of vertical columns used to support the various levels in Compact City are spaced further apart than the 20 feet usually found in conventional construction in order to further increase the feeling of openness, but not so wide apart that structural costs become prohibitive.

Density is a factor used to estimate the availability of space. Two-dimensional density is measured in people per square mile, and three-dimensional density is measured per cubic mile. It is interesting to note that if all the people in the world were placed at arm's length they would cover a plane of 625 square miles and if they were rearranged in layers eight feet apart, they would occupy less than one cubic mile.

The principle of space: in order to keep population densities low, conserve land use, and avoid the problems of urban sprawl, man must more effectively utilize the vertical dimension.

Compact city would be, according to the 1973 proposal, divided into five general spaces, each comprising a certain ring in the circular structure, from inside to outside, we would find:

> Core
> Core Edge
> Inner Residential Area
> Mid-Plaza
> Outer Residential Area

Compact City's work area is called the *Core*. Similar to the central commercial areas of present-day cities, the Core would contain offices, factories, warehouses, hospitals, high schools, and universities. Only heavy industry, such as blast furnaces and refineries, would be excluded from the Core area and located at some distance from the city. The Core shopping area would resemble some of the attractive covered shopping malls that are beginning to be built across the country today. The chief difference is that the proposed Core area would also include major hotels, convention halls, theaters, movies, sports facilities, as well as work, health, and education centers. The three-dimensional layout, of course, makes the areas used for these activities more readily accessible to one another – far more so than in the central core areas of a conventional city.

To revisit Safdie's paradox, this time in Dantzig and Saaty's words: "Just as people have a need to find escape from crowds, so also there appears to be the psychological need for people to gather closely together from time to time to socialize and engage in cultural activities. This is evidenced by voluntary attendance at sports events, at crowded night clubs and during intermission times at concerts and operas. The design proposed for Compact City may partially satisfy this need since people from all over the city would find it convenient to go to its gathering places in the centralized core area."

The Mid-Plaza is conveniently located between the Inner and Outer Residential Areas and provides local facilities such as elementary schools for children, clinics, neighborhood shops, parks, and play areas.

Part of the failure of the "Radiant City" approach to urban design is that it can, through its zoning off of various functions, isolate one area from its neighbor by permitting separating barriers of traffic and by using green space not for people but to make buildings look more attractive. It often creates lonely places where people have no defense against criminal attacks.

Some might criticize us by pointing out that we also propose to separate various functions in Compact City. For example, in the plan presented later in this chapter, residential areas are separated from work and commercial areas. There are, however, four important differences. First, there is the obvious one of ready accessibility of any part of the city to any other part. Second, the internal structures can be made less permanent. They could be made so they could be re-arranged to suit changing needs. Third, there would be greater stability of populations within a neighborhood because a change of jobs within the city would not require that a family move to another neighborhood; a family break-up would not mean a change in one's shopping patterns or schools. Fourth, considerable diversified use of interior open space is laid out in the plan.

Regarding transportation: In compact city, although electric-battery-powered cars would be available, distances would be so short that people would probably find it far more convenient to walk, bicycle, take an elevator, or ride the mass-transit system. In general, except for the transportation level accessible by elevators, there would be no wide streets in compact city but only wide alleys.

Walking should foster community life, because it is a natural way for people in a neighborhood to meet. People with similar interests could get to know each other while walking in the neighborhood or walking to a shopping center, a meeting, a sporting event, a theater, or a musical event. In this way common concerns of individuals could become known and translated into relevant community action. Such contacts are virtually impossible in today's cities because of the dependence on the automobile as a primary mode of transportation. Moreover, walking could contribute in a major way to public safety. Not only are pedestrians freer from accidents but active use of sidewalks provides some unstructured supervision of children and promotes the general security of the neighborhood against crime.

We could design the city so that the typical time (including walk time and wait time) to reach the Park-Roof or the mass transit on the middle level of the city from one's home or any part of the city would be about three minutes.

Suppose the city has grown to a maximum size and we are on the top level in the outer limits (Ring Z) and we wish to travel to a point diametrically opposite on the bottom level. The time to travel would be 12 minutes plus the time spent in waiting for the tram. Note that the "Core Exchange" area of the middle level serves as the main transfer point from one spoke route to another. We will assume that the mass transit cars are spaced two minutes apart so that the average waiting time would be one minute for any transfer.

Transportation throughout Compact City would be made easy by walking, bicycling, or by using the relatively simple mid-level mass transit system. Cars for use outside the city could be of conventional design and would be used for rides into the country or for trips between cities. Such cars would be parked at the periphery of the city. Because their use would be only occasional, they would probably be rented rather than owned. Driven by electricity, they would have a minimal role within the city.

To eliminate some of the roads on each level and to move up or down to a neighboring level for horizontal transportation on the roads there, would conserve space and considerably decrease the total size of the city. Crowding or interference problems occur in two dimensions because of the various types of flow paths for pedestrians. On the other hand, flow paths can be easily positioned in three dimensions so as to have no blocking or interference of one part of a network with another or of different networks with each other. In this connection, consider how much simpler the distribution of goods throughout the city might become. What once required a long time for transit between districts is now reduced to less than a minute by elevator to some desired vertical level. Little use remains for the millions of cars with their consequent pollution, accidents, manufacture, maintenance, and use. Public facilities, stadiums, and theaters become easily accessible to residents of all parts of the city. People would be able to live on the various horizontal layers closer to facilities than they would if all lived on the same horizontal plane. Transportation back and forth to work would no longer waste human time.

There are indirect costs associated with time spent in traveling. The time the principal wage earner needs to travel from his home to work and to return increases with city size and income level. A half hour each way, or one hour a day, is typical in today's large cities. In the New York area, however, it is not unusual for moderate-income wage earners to commute for one and a half hours each way or three hours a day. Because of the possibility of traffic tie-ups, most commuters allow extra travel time, say 15 minutes. Thus, total travel time for the principal wage earner varies between 1.25 and 3 or more hours per day.

There are other indirect costs due to an auto-based transportation system. For example, free parking lots around a shopping center are really not free but are paid for by the merchants within the center, who pass on that cost through increased prices for items shoppers purchase. Life insurance and health insurance rates include a cost to cover the possibility of highway accidents. There are indirect economic losses due to smog affecting natural foliage and human health. Then too, the wage earner is not the only person whose travel time constitutes an expense; travel time by other members of the household is growing, and most families can probably place a value on this time if it were freed for other uses. Finally, if the people presently earning their living in some aspect of automobile transport were eventually freed to perform other services in the economy, this could significantly increase the general standard of living

Today there are alternatives to the car and to transportation as we know them. In California, the smart driverless car is being tested. In other cities people are enticed to use modern efficient buses rather than driving their cars. Smartphones can be used in a multitude of ways to help people plan ahead and avoid delays.

The more effective use of the third dimension and the time dimension would reduce dramatically the number of people passing any particular point within the city at any particular time. All the parts of the city on any level would become easily accessible from any other level and any other part by foot, bicycle, car, or by the efficient mass transit system. Because of the continuity of activities around the clock, it is hard to imagine an occasion when one would ever encounter a fraction of the traffic congestion that characterizes present-day metropolises.

Another remarkable transportation opportunity afforded by the design of Compact City would be an automatic delivery system: Because of the effective use of the vertical dimension in the city, it would be feasible to install an automatic conveyor belt system for deliveries of small packages to and from houses and apartments. This conveyor system would be a convenient way of collecting solid wastes and recycling them economically.

An automatic delivery system, if combined with the water-recycling system to be discussed later, could be viewed as the analogue of the circulatory system, for the human body. It gives promise of a simpler way of life. Physically, the system would consist of a series of horizontal beltways on the middle level of the city; these would move objects to be delivered from distribution points to vertical belts which then raise or lower them to the house level where they would be finally deposited. A parallel system would work in the opposite direction. Many special services could be rendered in this way which is not now economically feasible. For example, food prepared in specialty kitchens could be sent directly to individual residences. Laundry could be sent out automatically and returned within, say, three hours – washed and dried. The automatic delivery system might also make convenient the rental of many things only occasionally used around the home. The automatic delivery system could supply any number of containers so that one would never need to mix the different types of trash but could keep them separate from each other at all times – a step considered essential in making recycling economically feasible.

Both present-day cities and Compact City require elaborate distribution networks, central facilities, and substations for electricity, communications, and water recycling. The installation costs are estimated to be lower in Compact City than in conventional cities because of shorter distance from the central input source of these utilities to the points of use; moreover, water pumping and transformer capacities would be lower in Compact City because of the more even distribution of demand through a 24-hour period.

A single three-dimensional urban environment is insulated from the outside, compared with present-day cities. The air conditioning system would be centralized in Compact City whereas in conventional cities individual homeowners must all purchase their own cooling equipment, furnaces, and air circulators. Because in Compact City all arcades, passageways, shopping centers, streets and many of the homes and gardens would be beneath the protective cover of the city roof, problems associated with rain, heat, and cold would not exist. There would be a significant decrease in the amount of energy needed to mostly cool the city year round. The city would be warm from all its internal activities and functions.

In Russia there are plans to build a glass-domed underground city by 2020. "The new city [will be] divided into three main levels with a vertical farm, forests, residences and recreational areas," said a spokesperson. "One of the most interesting aspects of the proposal is its glass dome. [It] will protect the city and be covered by photovoltaic cells that will harvest enough solar energy for the [whole] development." See the following link to the internet article: http://www.independent.co.uk/arts-entertainment/architecture/a-warren-of-streets-ecocity-2020-2149826.html.

Indeed, the structures within the city offer the most obvious examples of the great, almost paradoxical diversity granted by the all-encapsulating superstructure. Here is where the Compact City proposal reckons with those skeptical of total-system planning in general, represented most vehemently by Jane Jacobs.

According to Jane Jacobs, "city diversity itself permits and stimulates more diversity." Cities are "the natural homes of supermarkets and standard movie houses *plus* delicatessens, Viennese bakeries, foreign groceries, art movies and so on, all of which can be found coexisting—the familiar with the strange, the large with the small...This is because city populations are large enough to support wide ranges of variety and choice in these things. The diversity of whatever kind...rests on the fact that in cities so many people are so close together, and among them contain so many different tastes, skills, needs, supplies, and bees in bonnets."

Not only would the remarkable transportation opportunities grant access to greater diversity in Compact City, but its very nature would provide residents, planners and architects with a flexibility of design unheard of in buildings that need to reckon with exterior forces of weather, temperature, et cetera.

Thus the structures within the layered city could be constructed of light interior materials because the outer surface of the city itself could be built to provide the desired protection against the elements. Architecture could be infinitely more varied because of the greater choice of materials and architectural forms. Interior open space around homes and apartments would become useful areas of activity the year round. Streets need not be monotonously straight because transportation time is no longer a major problem.

In Compact City people would have a wide variety of choices of dwellings. These could be apartments or homes, large or small; they could vary greatly in style, and could be located on the exterior with a view of the surrounding country, or in the interior close to work or shopping. No matter where they are located, the Park-Roof or surrounding countryside is only a few minutes away. Most houses in Compact City would have two floors in order to conserve base area. Design of both the interior and exterior of these houses would vary according to the preferences of the residents. The ringway would provide access to the *rear* of the upper floor of a house. To facilitate home deliveries by electric-battery-powered trucks from the ringway, it would probably be convenient to have the upper floor of a house built to open directly onto the ringway. The lower floor, however could be offset 10 feet from the ringway 30 feet below, creating an appearance of openness and spaciousness there

The treatment of open space around homes and apartments in Compact City will probably be more utilitarian than in today's cities. In present-day suburbia the exteriors are largely decorative, making the neighborhood look nice with the least amount of upkeep. On the other hand, in Compact City the children will be able to play in the front yards and walkways without the danger of being run over because there are no streets or driveways there. Landscaping needs will also be different since (1) the entire city is immediately accessible to the rural environs and (2) it takes only a minute to reach the Park-Roof from any level. The vegetation around households in the interior of the city would, for practical reasons, be limited to foliage that can be maintained for long period under indirect or artificial light, and new ways would have to be found to make the interior open space around homes decorative with small waterfalls, rock gardens, colorful garden furniture. Because front yards will not be subjected to seasonal variations in climate, the outsides of houses will undoubtedly become a more integral part of the living space.

Today's exterior construction materials – concrete, stone, bricks, or cement blocks – are bulky, rough, heavy, and clumsy to handle. Once the many individual building units of a conventional urban development are finished, they are rigid and expensive to alter or replace. Whether we like it or not, what we build in a conventional city is what we are stuck with for several subsequent generations. By way of contrast, the only rigid part of Compact City would be its outer three-dimensional shell and the concrete slabs that form the "land" base for each level. The housing and work areas could be constructed upon these slabs and the terraces and parks could be planned in such a way as to permit easy modification and rearrangement. For example, lightweight less sturdy materials could be used to build the interior units. These could be designed to be mounted rapidly with ease and also to be dismounted and altered with effort that is small when compared with what is required to tear down or put up individual new building units in our current cities.

Houses could be made to be assembled rather than constructed, disassembled rather than wrecked. Parts of houses could be designed so that they could literally plug into each other. The same is true for office space, school rooms, and other arrangements within a neighborhood. The keynote of Compact City construction is its flexibility.

After living in a house for a while, the needs of the family can change but the family finds it easier to make the old home do, for exchanges are not easily arranged. If, finally, one must sell his home and relocate, this involves high agent fees, delays and location of temporary housing. The net result is that structures of a neighborhood remain as they were built; slowly they deteriorate into rotting, unattractive slums. The same is true for superblock projects – cities are stuck for a generation or two with what is constructed: society pays a high price for inflexible, rigid construction that is initially cheap.

The organization of the housing industry in Compact City, by way of contrast, could be built around the concept of change that could make it possible to redesign and rearrange homes, neighborhoods, work areas, and various other functions easily into new patterns to suit individual taste and changing community needs.

The roofs and exterior surfaces of houses could, if it is desired, be made of the same materials as the interior surfaces since there is no need for them to furnish protection against the rain or cold. Present-day technology is constantly developing new building materials. Light, sturdy, colorful heat- and sound-insulating materials of plaster board, plastic, or fiber glass would be particularly suitable modeled in various sizes and shapes so as to fit together perfectly and sturdily, and they could be made more attractive than most materials in common use today.

It would be a mistake, in the opinion of the author, to develop the interior open space around houses and apartment units the same way we develop the open space around suburban homes in present-day cities. Nature is more accessible in Compact City. The rural country-side would be only minutes away from any part of the city. Walking to work in natural settings could be accomplished by taking a route through the Park-Roof and this would add only a minute or two to the journey. The open spaces around the houses, because they are protected from the weather and from traffic danger, would probably be put to more functional uses.

It is possible that people would regard the exterior of a house as an extension of its interior, the chief differences being the degree of privacy and the increased ability to run around actively. Some interior rooms might be designed as four walls with an open ceiling and an archway opening onto the interior open space. By way of contrast, the open space in current suburbia is largely cosmetic. The landscaping is designed for easy upkeep and for making the neighborhood look nice. The sun, makes things grow; but this means that plants need to be trimmed, watered and weeded; and in the winter outdoor yards are bleak; at night and during hot summers outdoor areas may not be hospitable.

In Compact City the interior open space could be artificially lighted or sunlight could be brought in using the new fiber optic technology. If there is natural sunlight in the interior during the day plants requiring normal light can be used. Even artificially lighted lobbies of office buildings in conventional cities today are decorated with live plants. This is done by hiring a garden service that "recycles" the plants every few months, bringing in replacements that have been exposed to sunlight in fields and greenhouses.

Streets and houses would be lit in the usual way. The lights on vehicles would be used only in case of power failure. The lighting of the interior open space would, of course, be similar to that found in higher-ceilinged lobbies, banquet halls, convention centers, theaters, airports and railroad terminals. It is a creative exercise to improvise ways to bring sunlight anywhere in the city where it is desired to have it. We believe that this is possible with the new lighting technology of today. For example, fiber optics is the latest way to create indoor solar lighting. **Parans**, a Swedish company, collects sunlight outdoors and brings it inside using fiber optic cables. The ability to transport sunlight from outdoors inside has many benefits. Natural light encourages increased alertness. Productivity increases by 6 to 16 percent when natural light is added to a workplace. Sunlight gives improved visibility from improved light, better color rendering, and the absence of flickering from electrical lighting. Pure sunlight is dynamic and has a full spectrum that triggers the ganglion cells, which controls levels of melatonin and cortisol which is important for synchronizing the body clock. Solar lighting is environmentally friendly. To minimize depression, this author uses desk lamps both at home and at work which give off natural light like the sun.

Flood lights could be positioned to reflect light off ceilings. The undersides of levels could be sprayed with a material that reflects light and also absorbs sound. It would be desirable for its reflective properties to give a skyline appearance of distance.

It might also be useful to mention perhaps the most radical of the book's proposals—that of expanding our use of cities into the fourth dimension.

As space has become a premium in large cities, there has been a growing trend toward activities that operate more evenly around the clock. For example, there are restaurants that are always open, and taxicabs that are in use day and night. Some stores are open on some week nights or Sundays. It is becoming evident that this trend is desirable for an unencumbered way of life.

Such work schemes alleviate the pressures on traffic, communication, and recreation facilities. People use them during their free days- and these times do not coincide for all the people. By using three shifts in a 24-hour period, further reduction in total costs is achieved because the peak demands are smaller and more evenly distributed. It is evident that the structure of a city could be further improved if the times that people spend to work are distributed evenly throughout the day, night, weekdays, weekend, summer, and winter. Then there would be no peak periods of traffic, electricity, gas, shopping, clinics, restaurants, use of schoolrooms, use of factory equipment, etc. The result would be a great saving in the size and capacity of the capital stock as well as in the time and cost of new construction.

The principle of time: In order to conserve and maximize the effective use of space and to lead a less encumbered life, man needs to free himself from the syndrome of day-night cycles by utilizing the facilities of the city more evenly throughout the twenty-four hour day.

A summarizing list of the perceived advantages offered by Compact City:

1) Eliminates many of the inconveniences related to urban over-size.

2) Makes it possible to build a modern, convenient metropolis in a natural setting at a low cost, indeed, at costs which can be largely financed out of the savings now spent on transportation in present-day cities – on vehicles, accidents, roads, parking facilities, and gasoline.

3) Saves money. The preliminary analysis indicates that the cost for housing plus transportation for people with a moderate standard of living would be 25 percent less in Compact City than in present-day cities and would result in superior housing and superior transportation. The cost for good housing and transportation proposed for Compact City would run about 30 percent more than what people with a low standard of living presently are paying for poor housing plus poor transportation. For people presently enjoying a high standard of living, Compact City would cost 50 percent less for comparable housing and superior transportation. Moreover the expenditures for building Compact City represent a rechanneling of investments rather than a new burden. The cost of its construction should be weighed against the costs of further construction and renewal in today's cities, work that is outmoded before it is started.

4) Conserves the use of time. From one to three hours of time spent by wage earners in travel could be saved each day. Assuming 250 working days and $3.50 per hour wages, this amounts to a saving of from half a billion to one-and-a-half billion dollars of lost time each year in a

city of 600,000 wage-earners – a potential portal-to-portal income bonus of between 12 to 36 percent. Mother no longer would need to spend their time chauffeuring children. Distances are short and free from danger of accidents.

5) Saves lives. About 500 lives would be saved from death on highways and 6,000 accidents would be avoided each year in Compact City as compared to a present-day city, assuming both have 2,000,000 inhabitants. It would no longer be necessary to fence in yards or to engage in chauffeuring in order to protect children from being run over by cars.

6) Conserves the use of land. The city at maximum size could be built on less than nine square miles of land, whereas a comparable conventional city would require 178 square miles. The 170 square miles or so thus freed for use as farms or recreational areas would be within ten minutes distance of all the inhabitants of Compact City. Calculated at $1 per square foot, about $5 billion worth of land would be permanently preserved. In the next section we shall make a comparison with the use of land in present-day cities.

7) Makes it possible to locate the additional 70-100 million people who are expected to populate the United States, but without the destructive effect urban sprawl brings to the countryside, the environment, or the ecosystem.

8) Conserves the use of energy. Storing solar and other forms of energy through the use of mechanical storage for example the traditional pumping of water up and when needed, down by using turbines; through large fly

wheels with minimum friction and airless large chambers; by using fuel cells; or when technologically more improved, by using batteries. Water can be turned into ice that is used later in cooling. The redesign of the city would mean a different pattern of use of energy. In Compact City use of petroleum in autos and trucks would, of course, be dramatically reduced. So would direct use of petroleum for heating. On the other hand, there would be new needs: yards and interior open areas would need to be artificially lighted; air conditioning would be required to remove heat generated by people, lights, and appliances. Overall, there appears to be a reduction of energy use of at least 15 percent.

9) Conserves material resources. Automobile and gasoline costs per capita today in California run in the neighborhood of $500 per year. For an urban are with a population of two million, there are over one million cars. Transportation costs run over one billion dollars a year. As noted earlier, more than a million cars could be replaced by 10,000in Compact City. The round-the-clock use of facilities would drastically reduce the amount of equipment needed to handle peak loads. Installed equipment would be used more evenly and intensively. It would be renewed and modernized more often.

10) Has flexible construction that makes it possible for the city to easily adjust to changing needs. Present building methods are so rigid that it is not economical to relocate parts of the city or to modify existing parts. In contrast, the interior of Compact City would be protected from the weather so that less permanent construction could be

used. The need for flexible construction is extremely important in today's fast-moving world.

11) Could provide opportunities for the economically disadvantaged. Basically, because it is new and not bound by past customs, the city could provide a new start. In addition, educational and health facilities would become readily accessible to all because of the short distance involved.

12) Makes a city-wide automatic delivery system possible. Such a system might well have benefits for a city that are analogous to the function of arteries and veins in the human body. How the automatic delivery system could affect life in Compact City is discussed later.

13) Permits consolidation and centralization of certain urban services. Urban sprawl causes the duplication of hospitals, schools, and many other institutions. Later, we shall see that many specialized services that are not presently economically possible in cities because of time and distance could be made available in Compact City.

14) Makes it possible to have an ideal living environment almost anywhere. For example, if Compact City were located in a place with an extreme climate, large populations could live there – and thrive – in its comfortable interior climate while taking advantage of opportunities, economic or other, that might exist in the natural surroundings.

15) Eliminates air pollution. Because the atmosphere of Compact City would be controllable, air of the highest quality could, through better waste management,

recycling, and air filtering techniques, be in constant supply for all the inhabitants.

16) Makes possible economical water – and solid waste-recycling systems. The automatic delivery system can contribute to solid-waste disposal described in greater detail in the original book Compact City.

17) Reduces noise pollution and congestion because of the round-the-clock use of facilities, the less frequent use of cars, and the use of cars with battery power.

18) Decreases the suffering of people due to poverty and its effect on life. Left-over food would be delivered to special places where it would be available to the poor and needy.

Compact City proposes sweeping solutions to urban planning in a rapidly urbanizing world. Much of its original 1973 proposal, unfortunately perhaps, is still utterly relevant when considering alternatives to city design. Nor are these seemingly radical proposals to be written off as impossible. Governments, businesses and community organizations around the world are all attempting to answer pressing questions related to the way in which we build and live in the world. As T.S. Eliot said in these selected lines from "The Rock," T.S. Eliot (1934), and his words still ring true:

> *"What life have you if you have not life together?*
> *There is no life that is not in community . . .*
> *And now you live dispersed on ribbon roads*
> *And no man knows or cares who is his neighbor*
> *Unless his neighbor makes too much disturbance.*
> *But all dash to and fro in motor cars,*

Familiar with the roads and settled nowhere.
Nor does the family even move about together.
But every son would have his motorcycle,
And daughters ride away on casual pillions.
When the Stranger says: "What is the meaning of this
City?
Do you huddle close together because you love each
other?
What will you answer? 'We all dwell together
To make money from each other?' or 'This is a
community?' "

THE INNOVATIVE CITY NEEDS SMALLER ENTREPRENEURIAL ORGANIZATION

A study by Cai and Sit in Shanghai, one of the world's most innovative cities, indicates that its continued success is still an open question. The stakes and uncertainty are high as the city enters Stage 4 of the following City Development Life Cycle (CDLC):

Stage 1 is infrastructure building: attracting Multinational Enterprises (MNEs);

Stage 2 is cluster development: MNEs assuming cluster formation;

Stage 3 is MNEs dictating development;

Stage 4 is harmonious society: MNEs sharing corporate profits to ensure sustainable growth.

The Innovative CDLC model was used to frame the argument that despite the unprecedented pace of development in Chinese cities over the past decade, future economic progress in China may be increasingly constrained by limitations in the social structure that serve to attract skilled labor. The study came to a conclusion that innovations will need to be led by smaller entrepreneurial organizations, which would require a quite different focus from the one seen today. The basic idea is that ultimately, it is people who innovate.

WHAT IS AN ECO-COMPACT CITY?

An eco-compact city is a city developed in balance with the natural environment, with optimum population density and a rich system of small retail and an efficient public transit system. It is a pedestrian-friendly city. The Eco-Compact City Network (ECCN) was launched in 2008, aiming at "creating a forum for city officials, public and private developers, architects and engineers, to share the best examples of new ECC's and spread the culture of the ECC to create a better environment for the social, economic, and cultural life." (see: www.compactcity.org)

The ECCN categorizes the kinds of Eco-Compact Cities and characteristics they may have by giving the following examples:

ECO-COMPACT METROPOLIS: PARIS, FRANCE
It is a prominent city in terms of public function, with a population larger than a specific level (e.g., 1 million).

ECO-COMPACT CITY: SALAMANCA, SPAIN
It is physically organized according to a particular combination of open and built spaces, rich in facilities to satisfy the needs of social life of its residents. A city is an organic polycentric system of neighborhoods, districts, and villages.

ECO-COMPACT NEIGHBORHOOD: PLESSIS-ROBINSON, FRANCE

It is an organic part of a city with a certain functional and administrative autonomy and rich in public spaces (open and built). A Neighborhood includes a balanced system of activities: commercial, residential, productive, lodging, administrative, educational, and office.

ECO-COMPACT DISTRICT: AKROKEN CAMPUS, SWEDEN

It is an urban area specialized around a main activity, e.g., Theatre Districts, University Districts, Campuses, and Fair Districts. Its structure is similar to the one of Neighborhood, with an identified centre. The relationship with adjacent Urban Neighborhoods should encourage a pedestrian access. Districts should be interconnected through a system of public transit and located within the urban area.

ECO-COMPACT VILLAGE: POUNDBURY, UK

It is a small settlement of groups of buildings organically conceived as being dependent on a bigger urban centre. It is often considered to have a specific character, e.g., agricultural, industrial, marine, mining, or by a particular activity of its residents, such as a workers village or a youth village.

ECO-COMPACT PLAZA: PLAZA DE JUNKAL, SPAIN

It is an open public space organically connected with the surrounding urban fabric, providing a focal point for gathering. It hosts civic buildings such as town-halls, libraries, theatres, and churches.

ECO-COMPACT BLOCK: RUE DE LAKEN, BELGIUM

It is defined by buildings aligned on a street's edge, providing the block with one or several internal court yards where kids or elder people can play and rest in a protected green environment. It has a clear hierarchy between the external public space and the private or semi-private inner one.

ECO-COMPACT BUILDING: JANELAS VERDES, PORTUGAL
It is made of traditional regional materials expressing the climate, geographical, and cultural characters of the region. It is oriented towards the principles of bio-architecture, by using natural materials and construction techniques that minimize the consumption of energy.

GENERAL REQUIREMENTS AND PREFERENCES

Just as people have a need to find escape from crowds, so they also have a psychological need to gather closely together from time to time in order to feel insecure and estranged but a part of the population of the city. Gathering places should be accessible to people from all over the city, hence should be located in the centralized core area. It would even be desirable to make it possible for all the people to have access to the entire city.

To maintain its viability, a city must be supported by a productive population. A densely populated city could be designed for better living, accepting the population problem using the third dimension to release most of its agriculturally usable land. Inefficiencies need to be prevented by minimizing the distance and time of travel. Nature needs to be more available with minimum pollution.

Despite the general acceptance of compact cities, and despite the smallness and density in areas like England, France, Germany and

Italy, eastern China, Singapore, Japan, India Korea and others, there is a school of planners and demographers that speculate and argue that the trends today, rather than favoring the high-rise metropolitan city, in fact tend towards decentralization to small towns scattered throughout the country (the United States!).

They argue that the reasons for the existence of the central city are no longer there (think of New York, Paris, San Francisco and London?!). The need for the city as a transportation hub has been removed by the automobile and the highway (with all their problems and pollution); labor is highly mobile and is no longer dependent on heavy concentration of the population. Banking, whose money draws business, is now widespread to the smallest communities. Television and not-too-distant three-dimensional picture communication will make actual theatre and museum attendance obsolete. Small cities can be just as sufficient and satisfying as large cities, minus their frustrations. Rapid intercity transportation systems can move materials in and out of the city. Communication technology has made it increasingly unnecessary to travel or move about to see other people.

There seem to be questions about this argument. If people actually prefer electronic versions of large events, why do they still attend football games, with crowds of perhaps 100,000 people, rather than seeing the same event on their television set at home – free in most cases; or go to extraordinary lengths to attend a modern music concert? It is perhaps something in human psychology that causes most people to prefer to come together in groups, though the exact size of the group may be debatable.

Figure 4-1
(Source:http://en.wikipedia.org/wiki/File:Haifa_9568.JPG)

The presence of local supermarkets and shopping centers, satellite clinics, and nationwide divisions of business and industry with their jobs (perhaps shared by neighboring towns) diminish the need for living in the large city. Among the advantages of the small town are fresh air, sun, little or no crowding, easy access to nearby parks and recreation areas, and a more desirable social life with everybody acquainted with the people of the town.

Some ecologists prefer the linear city, stretching along a line to reduce the intensity of pollution on its inhabitants. At least in principle each house, rather than being surrounded, is only bordered on either side by other houses. It is also surrounded with parks and water bodies for recreation and to absorb falling pollution particles.

Figure 4-2 (Source: http://travel.webshots.com/photo/
2502506250091995847lnXWFP)

Protecting the environment and managing ecosystem services in future urban expansion requires purposeful management of space in advance of needs. Proactive policies for sustainability will also be important in view of climate change and the considerable proportion of urban concentrations at or near sea level.

City's life-support systems—clinics and hospitals, churches, schools, shopping areas, water, electricity, sewage and garbage services—need to be convenient and reasonably priced. They should be well integrated with the other systems. Sports, gardening, and other interaction with nature must be available and near. City life should be safe and loitering for mischief should be made more difficult.

COMPACT CITY AND QUALITY OF LIFE (QOL)

Efforts to explain quality of life (QOL) come from the interests of psychology, medicine, public health, economics, environmental sciences, sociology, and urban planning. Urban and regional policy makers believe that the character of the built environment is one of the many factors affecting QOL. The broad idea is that a certain spatial arrangement of an urban system would improve the QOL of its inhabitants by creating a new source of competitive advantage and promoting sustainability.

It is widely agreed that compact development cannot be avoided in ensuring sustainability and improving QOL of urban residents. Many empirical studies support compact development policies that would enhance city's competitive advantage and livability, which in turn would improve its residents' QOL. Empirical studies, however, still have not reached a consensus on the effect of compact development on QOL.

Aiming to provide healthy and productive places to live and work confronts cities in the developing world with challenges to meet rising demands for the necessary safe and respectable housing, transportation, water, waste treatment and other infrastructure and services. A study by Arifwidodo and Perera was conducted to explore a basic question of whether implementing compact city policies would significantly improve QOL of its residents. The study was conducted in Bandung, one of the highest growth cities in Indonesia, with 2.3 million people in 2007 and a density of 138 people per hectare. The finding suggests that there is no definite answer. Some compact development attributes appear to have positive effects, while others show negative effects that are less beneficial. The authors argue that although the findings cannot yet be generalized with confidence, the result seems to suggest that compact development policies applicable in developed countries may not be readily applicable to cities in developing countries. Cities in developing countries are more likely to face problems of managing the impact of intense compact development.

IDEAS FOR BUILDING COMPACT CITY

Housing in Compact City could be built around the concept of flexibility to make it possible to redesign and rearrange homes, neighborhoods, work areas, and various other functions easily.

The general plan of Compact City would open the interior views to give a feeling of spaciousness. This would be done with lighting, and with the setbacks, high ceilings, interior terraces, and decorative effects.

Figure 4-3 http://www.tophotelsoflondon.com/files/2012/09/
st_ermins_lobby01hdcooler_lo_res.jpg)

Figure 4-4 (Source: http://failuremagazine.blogspot.com/2010/04/
victor-gruens-shopping-mall.html)

Figure 4-5 (Source: http://www.agoda.web.id/asia/indonesia/bali
/hard_rock_hotel/reviews-page-2.html)

Houses are assembled rather than constructed, disassembled rather than wrecked. Parts of houses are designed to plug into each other. The same is true for office space, school rooms, and other arrangements within a neighborhood.

The "effective density" of the open space per person is less than in present day cities which means there is a greater degree of openness and free space.

Residences are along the ringways on both sides of the Mid-Plaza (center), where the local neighborhood shopping, elementary schools, nursery, clinic, and other local recreational facilities are all located. The roof and any upper levels have been cut away for this view in Figure 4-6.

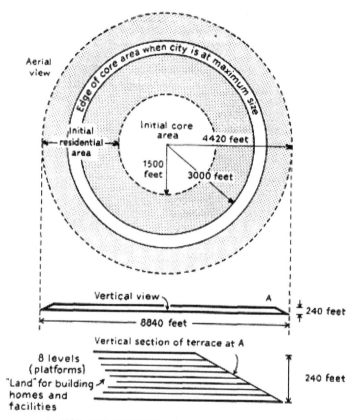

TOP AND SIDE VIEW OF COMPACT CITY

Population: 250,000. Base area: 2.2 square miles. As the city grows
to 2 million people, its height and diameter are expanded to
dimensions double those shown.

Figure 4-6 Top and side view of Compact City

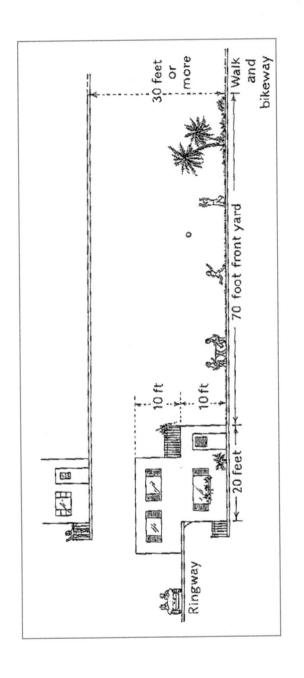

Figure 4-7 Two-story 2400-square-foot home with a spacious yard

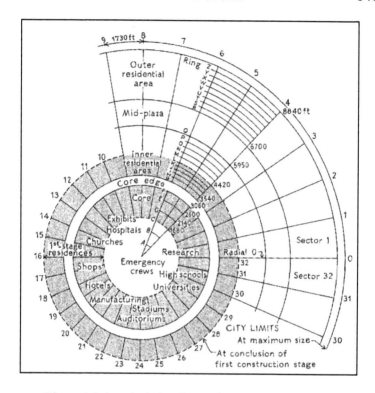

Figure 4-8 A typical plan for one level in Compact City

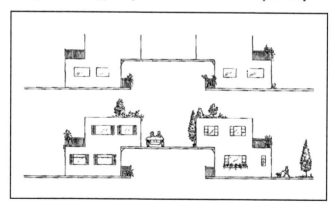

Figure 4-9 Setback of houses along a ringway

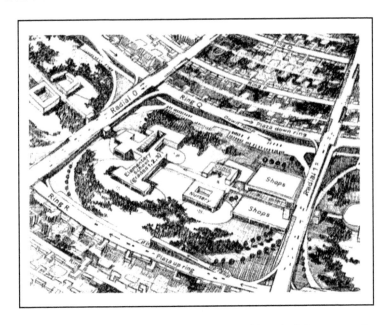

Figure 4-10 View of mid-plaza on a typical level of Compact City

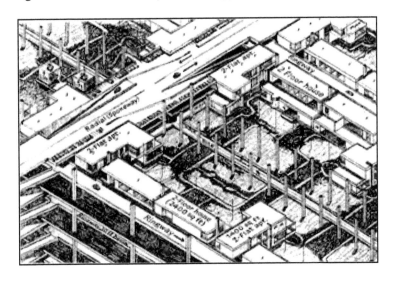

Figure 4-11 Detail of a residential section

Individual two-story houses and flats could vary greatly in style and design. Lots could vary in size also, though the average size would be 6,000 square feet. The city has eight levels, each level is separated from the next by at least 30 feet (with an increase to 16 levels as the city grows to maximum size).

Figure 4-12 The backs of homes face the ringway

Cars and trucks could make deliveries to the backs of homes, which open directly to the ringways as shown in Figure 4-12. At the top of the figure is the underside of a ringway. Note that from the lower floors of the houses, one can look over the next lower ringway. Because the front yards and walks are not in contact with the roadways, they are safe places to play.

4-13 Fronts of homes face the walkway-bikeway

4-14 View in a radial direction

Because the crosswalks pass over the roadways and have protective screens, they are safe for the pedestrian as shown in Figure 4-14

Figure 4-15 Children going to school

The walkway in the foreground leads to a 2-flat apartment complex. Cars travel along streets completely separated from places where people walk as shown in Figure 4-15. The safety of the walkways means that mothers would no longer need to spend time chauffeuring their children for fear of traffic accidents.

The vehicle shown in Figure 4-16 has (1) car platform at floor level, (2) easy to enter for children and wheelchairs, (3) no fare collection, (4) overhead suspension, (5) cushioned "cow-catcher' bumper, (6) capacity for 32 people, (7) safe shallow roadbed.

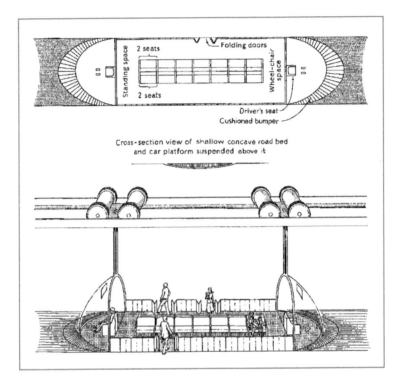

Figure 4-16 Mass transit car (tram)

The Core Exchange shown in Figure 4-17 is a large open lobby area in the center of the Core building at mid-level (Level 8). Mass transit trams converge from 32 radial directions to discharge their passengers at the edge of the open area and to start new runs (the front ends of four trams are visible near columns on the floor of the Core Exchange. The diameter of the Core Exchange is 250 feet. Tiered around it are theaters, hotels, restaurants, and shops. The supporting rim of a dome is at Level 14. Levels 14 to 16 would rise around the outside of the dome.

Figure 4-17 Core exchange (a cross-section view)

Packages are placed in standardized boxes and dispatched from any point in the city to any other point. The system shown in Figure 4-18 plays a role analogous in many ways to the arteries and veins of the human circulatory system. RFID (radio-frequency identification) tags would be an appropriate way to Identify and track the different packages just like in a large distribution center warehouse.

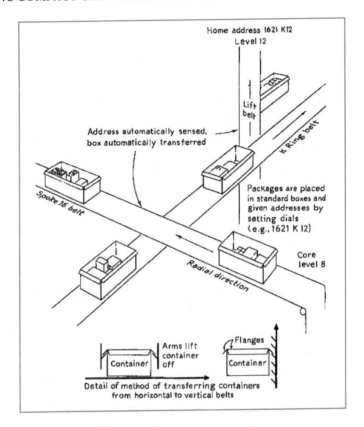

4-18 Automatic conveyor belt system

New York's Manhattan Island is an example of a high-density city. By contrast, Compact City at its maximum size would contain more people than Manhattan, would occupy one-third the area as shown in 4-19, be more convenient, have better access to business and recreational areas, and have an effective density that would make it one of the least dense cities in the world.

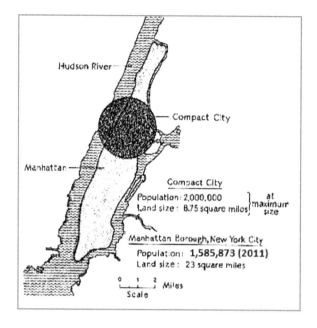

4-19 Compact City is one-third the size of Manhattan

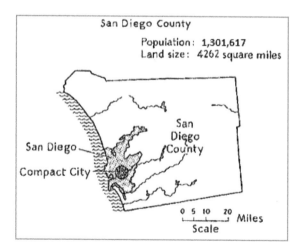

Figure 4-20 Compact City superimposed on San Diego

The nine square miles of Compact City could replace San Diego's sprawl of 4,262 square miles as shown in Figure 4-20.

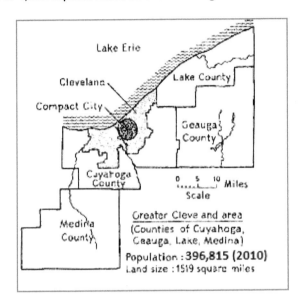

Figure 4-21 Compact City superimposed on Cleveland

The nine square miles of Compact City could replace Cleveland's four-county acreage as shown in Figure 4-21.

At one-tenth the size of Washington, DC, Compact City could absorb 1,400 square miles of urban growth that now spreads over three surrounding counties as shown in Figure 4-22.

Figure 4-22 Compact City superimposed on Washington, D.C.

Figure 4-23 A top view of Compact City

On the top of Compact City are a park roof and a conventional ring of apartments above the core area. The city is surrounded by rural countryside. The airport can be located close to the city because there are no suburbs.

Chapter 5

Multicriteria Decision Making

INTRODUCTION – THE NEED FOR HOLISTIC AND SEQUENTIAL DECISION MAKING

The evolution of our cities leads to the need to develop options of innovative designs or policies that would be beneficial for improving current conditions and providing us with opportunities to take advantage for future benefits and to choose the ones we want to go with. At the same time, we need to consider their cost and risk consequences too. We can only choose the best designs or policies by considering all the benefits-opportunities-costs-risks (BOCR) factors in a holistic manner. The Analytic Hierarchy Process (AHP), a theory for priority measurement for design and evaluation, created and developed by this author, is a way to make complex decisions involving feedback, and can be used to help with the many decisions and evaluations we need to make as we design our future cities.

We need not only to identify the BOCR elements, but also to understand interdependence among them and how the elements dominate each other to finally influence the outcome of our decision problem. Working with a group adds to the challenges but is inevitable to synthesize the diversity of knowledge and to deal with the difference in preferences.

The purpose of decision-making is to help people make decisions according to their own understanding. They would then feel that they really made the decision themselves justified completely according to their individual or group values, beliefs, and convictions even as one tries to make them understand these better. Because decision-making is the most frequent activity of all people all the time, the techniques used today to help people make better decisions should probably remain closer to the biology and psychology of people than to the techniques conceived and circulated at a certain time and that are likely to become obsolete, as all knowledge does, even though decisions go on and on forever. This suggests that methods offered to help make better decisions should be closer to being descriptive and considerably transparent. They should also be able to capture standards and describe decisions made normatively by following prescribed methods that appear to yield the best choice but overall may not. Natural science, like decision-making, is mostly descriptive and predictive to help us cope intelligently with a complex world.

We need the support of a decision making system that is not there simply to help us crunch numbers but also a framework that makes sense for organizing our understanding and ideas about the issues at hand, as well as our sense of priorities. We also need techniques to apply the framework that are scientifically valid yet relatively easy to apply by practitioners and decision makers to help them articulate their tacit visions and ideas as well as express and synthesize judgments of relative importance, both individually or collectively. We need a way that is based on how our brains work, rather than on telling us how it should be working.

The basic problem is that we need to quantify intangibles. We can only do it by making comparisons in relative terms. Even if everything were measurable, we would still need to compare the different types of measurements on the different scales and determine how important they are to us to make tradeoffs among them and reach a final answer. If we use tangibles and their measurements, we would need to reduce them to a common relative frame of reference and then weight and combine them along with intangibles. Combining priorities of measurable quantities with those of non-measurable qualities needs ratio or even the stronger absolute scales, because we can then multiply and add the outcomes particularly when there is interdependence among all the elements involved in a decision.

A decision-making approach should have the following characteristics:

1) Be simple in construct;
2) Be adaptable to use by both groups and individuals;
3) Be natural to our intuition and general thinking;
4) Encourage compromise and consensus building;
5) Not require inordinate specialization to master and communicate.
6) In addition, the details leading up to the decision-making process should be easy to review.

At the core of the problems that our method addresses is the need to assess the benefits, the opportunities, the costs and the risks of the proposed solutions. We must answer such questions as the following: Which consequences weigh more heavily than others? Which aims are more important than others? What is likely to take place? What should we plan for and how do we bring it about? These and other questions demand a multicriteria logic. It has been demonstrated over and over by practitioners who use the theory discussed in this paper, that multicriteria logic gives different and often better answers to these questions than ordinary logic and does it efficiently.

The set of potential outcomes and the alternatives from which to choose are the essence of decision making. In laying out the framework for making a decision, one needs to sort the elements into groupings or clusters that have similar influences or effects. One must also arrange them in some rational order to trace the outcome of these influences. Briefly, we see decision making as a process that involves the following steps:

1) Understand and define the problem as completely as possible

2) Structure a problem with a model that shows the problem's key elements and their relationships

3) Elicit judgments that reflect knowledge, feelings, or emotions

4) Represent those judgments with meaningful numbers

5) Use these numbers to calculate the priorities of the elements of the hierarchy

6) Synthesize these results to determine an overall outcome

7) Analyze sensitivity to changes in judgment

ASSESSMENT AND MEASUREMENT

Cities can be seen as complex networks of components: citizens, businesses, transports, communications, water, energy, city services, and other systems. City services integrate and coordinate the activities that take place in the other components. Understanding how activities improve and change through the lens of these elements offers cities new perspectives on the progress they are making toward implementing their strategies for achieving their objectives.

The performance of core systems of today's cities is fundamental to social and economic progress. As the world becomes increasingly instrumented, interconnected, and intelligent in nature, new smart solutions and management practices are available for cities to use to help them accelerate their journey towards sustainable prosperity. The application of smart solutions could improve and optimize their core systems to cope with today's major challenges.

As an example, Van Assche reported on the use of the City Monitor, a policy instrument to measure development progress of 13 Flemish cities. As many as 200 experts from city governments and other administrations, as well as civil society and the academic world were involved. The instrument was meant to provide feedback for urban policy debate about QOL in those cities, using the indicators that were constructed based on a normative vision about sustainability. The participative or co-design approach was used to capture uncertainty, complexity, and the value base of the cities involved. They came up with about 200 livability and sustainability indicators that would need to be simplified to be useful.

The IBM Institute for Business Value maintains that it is essential to assess a city's core systems and activities. Such an assessment, ideally, should be:

1) Tailored to support insights around achieving the city's specific vision and strategy to drive sustainable prosperity;

2) Holistic, covering all the systems that make up the city;

3) Comprehensive in capturing how performance would change based on introduction of new 'smarter' solutions;

4) Comparative, to allow benchmarking the city's performance against relevant peer cities.

In devising an instrument to measure the progress in development, most researchers still use the conventional method that is not supported by a scientific measurement theory. For example, Cai and Sit devised a rating method to evaluate world city formation using quantifiable indicators to generate world city index, and six interdependent dimensions with 22 attributes (4 ordinal, 18 ratio). The use of the City Monitor instrument, as Van Assche reported, was still posing a challenge to how to integrate different community needs and various urban policies. This suggests that the 200 indicators were not developed using a structure showing the interdependency between the needs and policies that would help urban authorities to analyze such integration.

Today almost 80 percent of Europe's population live and work in urban agglomerations. In response to the urgent need for solutions to deal with the current ongoing challenges, the European Commission (EC) introduced Urban Europe in 2008, a new Joint Programming Initiative (JPI) to promote country members' collaboration on research intended for creating attractive, sustainable and economically viable urban areas.

"The vision of the JPI, 'URBAN EUROPE' (formerly: Future of Cities & Transport – FoCIT), is to fundamentally rethink and manage the dynamics of urban development in Europe to sustain and enhance urban areas as a place of vitality, livability, and accessibility. To reach these aims URBAN EUROPE provides a systemic approach which takes utmost advantage of emerging technologies by assessing their potential and socio-economic impacts and utilizing them in new urban policies and design strategies.

JPI's main aim is to coordinate research and make better use of Europe's public funds in order to:

1) Transform urban areas to centers of innovation and technology
2) Realize eco-friendly and intelligent intra-en interurban transport and logistics system
3) Ensure social cohesion and integration
4) Reduce the ecological footprint and enhance climate neutrality."

See http://www.jpi-urbaneurope.edu/ for the above quoted material.

The Analytic Hierarchy Process (AHP) and its generalization to dependence and feedback, The Analytic Network Process (ANP) comprise a well-known methodology that has been widely used for making the same kind of complex decisions needed here for choosing among the kind of cities to build, their design, location and all the nuances involved in trading off different characteristics. Here we introduce this decision support method and show some examples of how it can be applied.

The AHP is about breaking a problem down, prioritizing all the factors and then aggregating the solutions of all the sub-problems into a conclusion. It facilitates decision making by organizing perceptions, feelings, judgments, and memories into a framework that identifies and exhibits the forces that influence a decision. In the simple and most common case, the forces are arranged from the more general and less controllable to the more specific and controllable. The AHP is based on the innate human ability to make sound judgments about small problems. It has been applied in a variety of decisions and planning projects in nearly 20 countries.

Most important decisions involve a number of criteria which the alternatives of choice must satisfy, more or less. To rank cities overall we must first decide what the criteria will be and then rank the cities under each criterion. The various rankings must then be combined to give an overall rank. There is a method of multi-criteria decision making that can be used to do this, the Analytic Hierarchy Process (AHP), which this author developed during the years the original Compact City book was published.

The connections between the factors that go into making a decision have two kinds of structures. The first is hierarchic descending from a goal to criteria, subcriteria, then down to a level of alternatives that need ranking to determine the best choice. The other kind of structure is a network with inter-dependencies and feedback. The Figure 5-1 and Figure 5-2below illustrate these two structures.

We start by dealing with hierarchical decision making structures to give the reader familiarity with making these kinds of decisions. We leave it to the reader to consult the books written by this author about networks and their applications in a large diversity of governmental, private enterprise and personal problems.

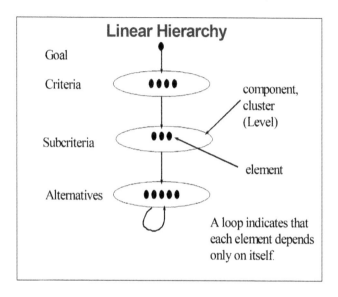

Figure 5-1 A general hierarchy

A hierarchy, as shown in Figure 5-1, assumes that influence flows from the top element of overall goal to the bottom elements or alternatives through the levels in between.   There is no dependence between lower level elements on those in the higher level. For example, in a multi-criteria selection problem, the relative importance of the criteria determines the relative priority or preference of the alternatives. The relative intensity of the set of criteria that characterize the alternatives does not determine the relative importance of the criteria.   A hierarchy also assumes that elements in the same level are independent from each other.

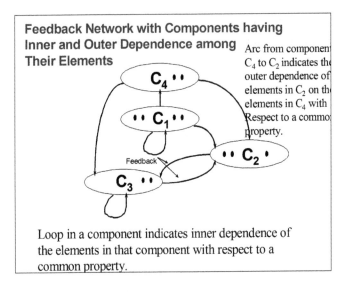

Feedback Network with Components having Inner and Outer Dependence among Their Elements

Arc from componen C_4 to C_2 indicates th outer dependence of elements in C_2 on th elements in C_4 with Respect to a commo property.

Feedback

Loop in a component indicates inner dependence of the elements in that component with respect to a common property.

Figure 5-2 A general network

An Analytic Network Process (ANP) decision model, shown in Figure 5-2, is a more general structure that allows connections in other ways than the top down ones in a hierarchy. An ANP model is better for capturing the complexity of the real world. the elements, the dots in the figure, are grouped into components or clusters, the oval shapes. In a network, unlike in a hierarchy where connections go from the top down, there can be inner dependence among the elements in a cluster; the loops represent inner dependent connections, and there can be feedback with the connections between the elements in two clusters going both ways.

In this chapter we will explain the ideas in some detail and illustrate with examples. Decision making requires measuring alternatives in some way. If there are existing scales for the various criteria they can be used, but often there are no scales and we are dealing with intangible properties, so a scale needs to be constructed first that we will use to measure the alternatives on each of the criteria. Here what Plato said is of a major concern: "The art of measurement would do away with the effect of appearance ... they err not only from defect of knowledge in general, but of that particular knowledge which is called measuring." We will show how the AHP facilitates the process to produce a valid outcome.

PAIRED COMPARISONS AND THE 1-9 FUNDAMENTAL SCALE

Comparing is a natural process that people are able to do to express their sense of preference, importance, or likelihood with respect to a common objective or property they have in mind. Paired comparisons are the way to do it most accurately. This is the first fundamental paradigmatic shift of the AHP in conceptualizing how the mind works to generate judgments or expression of such sense of relative priority and order. Judgments involving both tangibles and intangibles are inherently subjective. Even tangible qualities might mean different things to different people; hence the idea of constructing a utility function, an absolute scale to convey a subjective sense of importance. Despite the difficulty in applying the utility approach, it is clear that one will never be able to construct a valid utility function based on a discrete number of judgments. Hence it is unrealistic to try to measure intangibles in absolute terms, in the same way as what has been used for tangibles, simply because intangible means "no absolute definition possible". The AHP applies relative measurement, the only way to measure intangibles for understanding.

Consequently, to construct a measurement theory that would be applicable in complex problems, a new scale had to be invented to represent relative judgments. To make a judgment on a pair of elements, start by deciding which element is dominant in the pair to be judged, and then select a verbal expression that best expresses how dominant it is.

Equal importance
Moderate importance of one over another
Strong or essential importance
Very strong or demonstrated importance
Extreme importance

Note that here we attempt to provide our honest judgment, not arbitrary like saying: the sun is extremely larger than an apple or even that a watermelon is extremely larger than a grape. It has been generally agreed that our mind can only compare two things relatively accurately within an order of magnitude hence that is what we mean by "extreme importance." Moreover, we generally need to compare more than a pair of objects, which calls for converting the verbal judgments into numbers so that they can be synthesized to derive their relative measurement. Pursuing the accuracy of their representation demands that they need to be validated when measurements exist to enhance the belief that accurate outcomes can also be reaches by experts when applying judgment to compare intangibles.

The AHP uses the integers 1 to 9 as its Fundamental Scale of Absolute Numbers corresponding to the verbal statements for the comparisons. This scale is **not** an arbitrarily chosen set of ordinal numbers but is a meticulously and mathematically derived scale of absolute numbers by using stimulus-response theory in psychology.

1 Equal importance
3 Moderate importance of one over another
5 Strong or essential importance
7 Very strong or demonstrated importance
9 Extreme importance
Use 2,4,6,8 for intermediate values and reciprocals for inverse comparisons

The mathematician and cognitive neuropsychologist, Stanislas Dehaene (1997) writes in his book, The Number Sense, How the Mind Creates Mathematics:

> "Introspection suggests that we can mentally represent the meaning of numbers 1 through 9 with actual acuity. Indeed, these symbols seem equivalent to us. They all seem equally easy to work with, and we feel that we can add or compare any two digits in a small and fixed amount of time like a computer."

THE BASIC STRUCTURE: A HIERARCHY OF TWO LEVELS WITH A JUDGMENT MATRIX

In its simplest form the AHP provides a priority measurement tool in a simple 2-level hierarchical structure. The single top element above represents a common property and the elements in the second level represent the set of alternatives to be pairwise compared with respect to the common property. Our problem is to estimate the relative sizes (volume) of three apples A, B, and C, using AHP in the two-level hierarchy shown in Figure 5-3.

A judgment or comparison is the numerical representation of a relationship between two elements that share a common parent. The set of all such judgments can be represented in a square matrix in which the set of elements is compared with itself. Each judgment represents the dominance of an element in the column on the left over an element in the row on top.

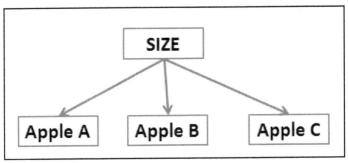

Figure 5-3 Two-level hierarchy for comparing apple sizes

Let us denote S_1, S_2, and S_3 as the actual sizes in volume of apples A, B, and C respectively, then we can construct a pairwise comparison matrix as shown in Table 5-1.

Table 5-1 Pairwise comparison matrix

Size Comparison	Apple A	Apple B	Apple C
Apple A	S_1/S_1	S_1/S_2	S_1/S_3
Apple B	S_2/S_1	S_2/S_2	S_2/S_3
Apple C	S_3/S_1	S_3/S_2	S_3/S_3

Without knowing their actual sizes, we will be able to provide a judgment that is an estimate of the ratio of the sizes of two apples, S_1/S_2, in answer to the question: given Apple A and Apple B, how many times is Apple A (the bigger one) larger when compared with Apple B (the smaller one)? Our mind works more naturally to judge how much bigger an object is relative to a smaller one than the other way around. So the smaller apple serves as the unit and the judgment is how many multiples of that unit is the larger apple. Note the reciprocal property of each pairwise comparison, i.e., if Apple A is S_1/S_2 times bigger than Apple B, then Apple B is S_2/S_1 smaller than Apple A. The pairwise comparison judgments can be expressed by using either a verbal statement or its numerical representation by using the AHP Fundamental Scale, but the number is entered in the appropriate cell in the matrix. Note that only the judgments above the diagonal need to be entered because those below the diagonal are reciprocals of the ones above. We apply the scale and obtain the pairwise comparison matrix shown in Table 5-2.

Table 5-2 Pairwise comparison matrix with judgments

Size Comparison	Apple A	Apple B	Apple C	Resulting Priority Eigenvector	Relative Size of Apple
Apple A	1	2	6	6/10	A
Apple B	1/2	1	3	3/10	B
Apple C	1/6	1/3	1	1/10	C

When the judgments are consistent, as they are here, any normalized column gives the priorities.

For a set of n elements in a matrix one needs $n(n-1)/2$ comparisons because there are n ones on the diagonal (for comparing elements with themselves) and of the remaining judgments, half are reciprocals. Thus we have $(n^2- n)/2$ judgments. In some problems one may elicit only the minimum number (n -1) of judgments. From all the paired comparisons we calculate the priorities, obtained mathematically by deriving the principal eigenvector of the matrix. In general our judgments are not consistent hence their normalized column would not give the same number. Column normalization is the process of dividing the numbers in a column with the total sum of the numbers in that particular column. The normalized numbers in that column would then add up to 1. The principal eigenvalue of the judgment matrix is used in calculating the amount of inconsistency of our judgments. For a completely consistent matrix, the eigenvalue is equal to n, the size of the matrix (e.g., 3 for our apple comparison matrix).

In the foregoing example Apple B is 3 times larger than Apple C. We can obtain this value directly from the comparisons of Apple A with Apples B & C as 6/2 = 3. But if we were to use judgment we may have guessed it as 4. In that case we would have been inconsistent. Now guessing it as 4 is not as bad as guessing it as 5 or more. The farther we are from the true value the more inconsistent we are. The AHP provides a theory for checking the inconsistency throughout the matrix and allowing a certain level of overall inconsistency but not more, and also identifying the most inconsistent judgments and asking people if, according to their understanding, they are willing to change their mind by a certain amount, not necessarily that recommended by the computer program. If the inconsistency remains high, no decision can be made without further study and improved understanding.

People are inherently inconsistent, which is generally perceived as a weakness but actually being somewhat inconsistent is an essential quality for the mind to allow us to grow intellectually by learning new ideas that cause us to modify the relationships among what we already know. Unfortunately, most theories and methods proposed for priority measurement and decision making have been developed with an underlying assumption that people are consistent. It is thought that a proposed method might produce an outcome that accurately captures the underlying priority in the mind of the decision maker. We maintain that this is not necessarily the case. Assuming consistent judgments might lead to an unreliable outcome. Lack of understanding of this inconsistency phenomenon could lead either to a misleading action, assuming a reliable outcome, or ignoring the result hence making the method useless.

Effective decision making needs coherent thinking to be reliable. Here we need to define coherence as an acceptable level of inconsistency rather than perfect consistency. The level of inconsistency of a set of judgments can be used as a measure of their accuracy in representing the underlying sense of priority. Using a way of thinking that *it is better to be approximately right than precisely wrong*, the AHP introduced a way to strive for reasonable accuracy by requiring some redundancy in judgments and producing an inconsistency index as a measure of how accurate the outcome represents the synthesis of the true set of judgments in the mind of the user with regard to the problem being considered.

EVALUATING INHOMOGENEOUS OBJECTS

The 1 to 9 scale is only applicable in comparing a set of homogeneous objects, i.e., their relative sizes are within one order of magnitude, as one must not have more than seven elements in a comparison set because of the likelihood of increasing inconsistency beyond acceptable limits. If we have more than seven, we can divide them into groups of homogeneous elements with pivots. A pivot is a common element between one group and the next. Below we show how to compare the size of a watermelon to a cherry tomato, with three sets of pairwise comparison judgments, repeating a pivot element from one set to the next as shown in Figure 5-4.

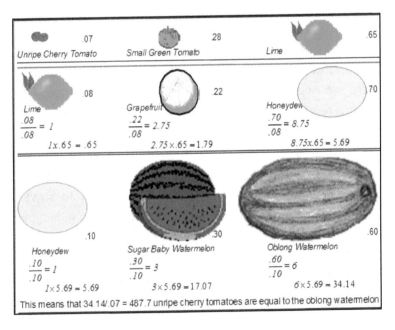

Figure 5-4 Expanding the 1-9 scale to inhomogeneous objects

The 1–9 scale can be validated by comparing the outcome of applying the scale to a set of tangible objects with its actual numbers. Here is an example of estimation where the answer can be checked against known data: Which drink is consumed more in the U.S.? The judgments, given by a group of graduate students, who were able to estimate reasonably well, are shown in Table 5-3 below.

Table 5-3 Estimating relative consumption of drinks using judgments

Drink Con-sumption	Coffee	Wine	Tea	Beer	Sodas	Milk	Water	Wts
Coffee	1	9	5	2	1	1	1/2	0.177
Wine	1/9	1	1/3	1/9	1/9	1/9	1/9	0.019
Tea	1/5	3	1	1/3	1/4	1/3	1/9	0.042
Beer	1/2	9	3	1	1/2	1	1/3	0.116
Sodas	1/1	9	4	2	1	2	1/2	0.190
Milk	1/1	9	3	1	1/2	1	1/3	0.129
Water	2	9	9	3	2	3	1	0.327

Inconsistency 0.022

The derived scale is obtained by calculating the eigenvector and its consistency ratio of 0.022 is calculated from the associated eigenvalue. The AHP is supported by the *SuperDecisions* software (available from www.superdecisions.com) that facilitates its application and the calculations.

The estimated relative consumption of drinks is given by the solution vector of the above matrix (the eigenvector), the relative weights. For an interpretation of relative weights consider that Sodas have a weight of 0.190 and Tea has a weight of 0.042. The result of dividing 0.190/0.042 = 4.53, which means 4.53 times as many sodas are consumed as tea. The matrix has a consistency ratio of 0.022 which is well under the suggested limit of 0.1.

The estimated relative consumption of drinks, the AHP solution, is given in the first row in Table 5-4. The actual relative consumption of drinks, taken from the US statistical tables, is given in row two. Note the close agreement.

Table 5-4 Estimated (first row) versus actual relative consumption of drinks

Coffee	Wine	Tea	Beer	Sodas	Milk	Water
.177	.019	.042	.116	.190	.129	.327
.180	.010	.040	.120	.180	.140	.330

This example, along with numerous others that have been done over the years, shows that knowledgeable people have the ability to judge in relative terms with reasonably good accuracy. This inborn ability is useful for comparing intangibles, and by using it in conjunction with the Fundamental Scale and hierarchical structures of the AHP it is possible to analyze complex problems.

THE KEY TO APPROACHING A COMPLEX PROBLEM: STRUCTURE IT AS A MODEL

Perhaps the most creative part of decision making that has a significant effect on the outcome is modeling the problem. In the AHP, a problem is structured as a hierarchy. In the Analytic Network Process (ANP), one structures a problem as a network of clusters of related elements. It is then followed by a process of prioritization, which we have already seen in the apple size comparison example. We now know that prioritization involves eliciting judgments in response to questions about the dominance of one element over another when compared with respect to a property. The basic principle to follow in creating this structure is always to see if one can answer the following question: "Can I compare the elements on a lower level using some or all of the elements on the next higher level as criteria or attributes of the lower level elements?"

A useful way to proceed in structuring a decision is to come down from the goal as far as one can by decomposing it into the most general and most easily controlled factors. One can then go up from the alternatives at the bottom beginning with the simplest subcriteria that they must satisfy and aggregating the subcriteria into generic higher level criteria until the levels of the two processes are linked in such a way as to make comparison possible.

Here are some suggestions for an elaborate design of a hierarchy:

(1) Identify the overall goal. What are you trying to accomplish? What is the main question?

(2) Identify the sub-goals of the overall goal. If relevant, identify time horizons that affect the decision.

(3) Identify criteria that must be satisfied to fulfill the subgoals of the overall goal.

(4) Identify sub-criteria under each criterion. Note that criteria or sub-criteria may be specified in terms of ranges of values of parameters or in terms of verbal intensities such as high, medium, low.

(5) Identify the actors involved.

(6) Identify the actors' goals.

(7) Identify the actors' policies.

(8) Identify options or outcomes.

(9) For yes-no decisions, take the most preferred outcome and compare the benefits, opportunities, costs, and risks of making the decision with those of not making it.

(10) Do a (benefit × opportunity)/(cost × risk) analysis using marginal values. Because we are dealing with dominance hierarchies, ask which alternative yields the greatest benefit and opportunities; for costs and risks, which alternative costs the most, and for risks, which alternative is more risky.

To make a decision by considering benefits and costs, one must first answer the question: In this problem, do the benefits justify the costs? If they do, then either the benefits are so much more important than the costs that the decision is based simply on benefits, or the two are so close in value that both the benefits and the costs should be considered. Then we use two hierarchies for the purpose and make the choice by forming the ratio from them of the (benefits priority/cost priority) for each alternative. If the benefits do not justify the costs, the costs alone determine the best alternative, that which is the least costly.

There are two ways to structure an AHP model. The first is relative decision making in which the criteria are compared for their importance with respect to the goal and the alternatives are compared against each other for preference with respect to each criterion using the AHP fundamental scale to make the judgments. The second uses absolute measurement in which the alternatives are evaluated one at a time using standardized scales for each criterion. We illustrate the two methods below on the decision of choosing a best city to live in.

PICKING A BEST CITY TO LIVE IN USING THE RELATIVE MEASUREMENT MODE OF AHP

The AHP model for picking a best city in which to live is shown below in Figure 5-5. The person making this decision is a native of Pittsburgh, with family who live near the city.

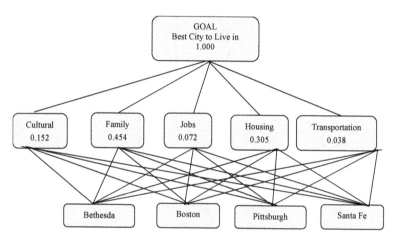

Figure 5-5 AHP model for picking a best city to live in

ENTERING JUDGMENTS FOR THE CRITERIA

A square matrix is constructed for the comparisons with the criteria listed for the rows and the columns. One answers this question for the cell: How much more important is the row element than the column element in choosing a best city? The judgments, shown in Table 5-5, are entered using the Fundamental Scale of the AHP. For example, for the (Culture, Housing) cell the value 3 is entered meaning Culture is moderately more important than housing. The inverse judgment 1/3 is automatically assigned for the converse judgment (Housing, Culture). Fractional values between the integers 4 and 5, such as

4.32, can also be used when they are known from measurement, or when the judge thinks he/she is sufficiently perceptive.

Table 5-5 Criteria weights with respect to the goal

Goal	Culture	Family	Housing	Jobs	Transport-ation	Priorities
Culture	1	1/5	3	1/2	5	0.152
Family	5	1	7	1	7	0.433
Housing	1/3	1/7	1	1/4	3	0.072
Job	2	1	4	1	7	0.305
Transport-ation	1/5	1/7	1/3	1/7	1	0.038

Inconsistency 0.05

THE NUMBER OF JUDGMENTS REQUIRED AND CONSISTENCY

In this decision there are 10 judgments to be entered. As we shall see later, inconsistency for a judgment matrix can be computed as a function of its maximum eigenvalue λ_{max} and the order n of the matrix. The time gained, from making fewer judgments than 10 along a spanning tree for example can be offset by not having sufficient redundancy in the judgments to fine tune and improve the overall outcome. There can be no inconsistency when the minimum number of judgments is used.

Next the alternatives are pairwise compared with respect to each of the criteria. The judgments indicate the decision maker's preference, given a pair of alternatives to judge with respect to each of the criteria, as shown in the five matrices in Table 5-6.

.

The priority vector shown for each matrix is obtained by computing its principal eigenvector. To get an approximation to the eigenvector, sum across each row and normalize the resulting sums to either: 1) the distributive form (shown in the tables) by totaling them and dividing by the total so they then sum to 1.0, or 2) the ideal form by dividing each by the largest of them, so the best, or ideal, gets a value of 1. Inconsistency should be less than 0.10.

Table 5-6 Five matrices containing the judgments

Culture	Bethesda	Boston	Pittsburgh	Santa Fe	Priorities
Bethesda	1	½	1	1/2	0.163
Boston	2	1	2.5	1	0.345
Pittsburgh	1	½.5	1	1/2.5	0.146
Santa Fe	2	1	2.5	1	0.345

Inconsistency = .002

Family	Bethesda	Boston	Pittsburgh	Santa Fe	Priorities
Bethesda	1	2	1/3	4	0.210
Boston	1	1	1/8	2	0.098
Pittsburgh	3	8	1	9	0.635
Santa Fe	¼	½	1/9	1	0.057

Inconsistency = .012

Housing	Bethesda	Boston	Pittsburgh	Santa Fe	Priorities
Bethesda	1	5	1/2	2.5	0.262
Boston	1/5	1	1/9	1/4	0.047
Pittsburgh	2	9	1	7	0.571
Santa Fe	1/2.5	4	1/7	1	0.120

Inconsistency = .012

Jobs	Bethesda	Boston	Pittsburgh	Santa Fe	Priorities
Bethesda	1	½	3	4	0.279
Boston	2	1	6	8	0.559
Pittsburgh	1/3	1/6	1	1	0.087
Santa Fe	¼	1/8	1	1	0.075

Inconsistency = .004

Transport-ation	Bethesda	Boston	Pittsburgh	Santa Fe	Priorities
Bethesda	1	1.5	1/2	4	0.249
Boston	1/1.5	1	1/3.5	2.5	0.157
Pittsburgh	2	3.5	1	9	0.533
Santa Fe	¼	½.5	1/9	1	0.061

Inconsistency = .001

SYNTHESIZE TO GET THE ANSWER

The outcome using the distributive form is shown in Table 5-7. "Distributive form" means the priorities in each column sum to 1.0. To synthesize to obtain the overall priorities, multiply each row entry by the criterion value and sum across the row to get the totals. If the Totals don't sum to 1.0, normalize them to get the overall priorities, but in the case of the distributive mode the totals are already normalized.

Table 5-7 Distributive synthesis of Overall City Priorities

Syn-thesis	Cultural 0.152	Family 0.433	Housing 0.072	Jobs 0.305	Transpt 0.038	Totals (Weight and add)	Overall Priorities (Norm. Totals)
Bethesda	0.163	0.210	0.262	0.279	0.249	0.229	0.229
Boston	0.345	0.098	0.047	0.559	0.157	0.275	0.275
Pittsburgh	0.146	0.635	0.571	0.087	0.533	0.385	0.385
Santa Fe	0.345	0.057	0.120	0.075	0.061	0.111	0.111

To change the distributive form of the columns shown in Table 5 into the ideal form, divide each entry in the column by the largest element in the column. The "ideal" city for each criterion has a priority of 1.000. The ideal forms are shown in Table 5-8. Then multiply and add as before, but in this case the Totals must ben normalized to give the Overall Priorities.

Table 5-8 Ideal Synthesis

Synth-esis	Cultur-al 0.152	Fam-ily 0.433	Hous-ing 0.072	Jobs 0.305	Trans-port 0.038	Totals (Weight and add)	Overall Priorities (Normal-ized Totals)
Bethesda	0.474	0.330	0.459	0.500	0.467	0.418	0.224
Boston	1.000	0.155	0.082	1.000	0.295	0.541	0.290
Pittsburgh	0.424	1.000	1.000	0.155	1.000	0.655	0.351
Santa Fe	1.000	0.089	0.209	0.135	0.115	0.251	0.135

The final outcome using either type of synthesis is that Pittsburgh is the highest ranked city for this individual. Though the final priorities are somewhat different, the order is the same. The cities and their priorities in the distributive mode are: Pittsburgh (0.385), Boston (0.275), Bethesda (0.229), and Santa Fe (0.111). The ratios of the final priorities are meaningful. Pittsburgh is almost twice as preferred as Bethesda, and 4 times as preferred as Santa Fe.

Another way to interpret this is that out of 100 people making such a decision, with similar criteria, 38.5 choose Pittsburgh, 27.5 choose Boston, 22.9 choose Bethesda and 11.1 choose Santa Fe.

In the distributive mode of synthesis Pittsburgh has an overall priority of 0.385, Boston is number two at (0.275), Bethesda is number 3 at (0.229) and Santa Fe is number 4 at (0.111). It is easy to see why Pittsburgh is the best choice because Family is the most important criterion with almost half the priority at 0.433 and Pittsburgh has the highest priority of 0.635 for Family, so it is the overall winner.

An important distinction to make between measurement in physics and measurement in decision-making is that in physics we usually seek measurements that approximate to the weight and length of things, whereas in human action we seek to order actions according to priorities. In mathematics a distinction is made between *metric topology* that deals with the measurement of length, mass and time and *order topology* that deals with the ordering of priorities through the concept of *dominance* rather than closeness used in metric methods. We have seen that the principal eigenvector of a matrix is necessary for capturing dominance priorities.

Another thing to notice about measurement in physics is that it is based on previously established scales so the process is that one measures first, getting a number from the scale, then it takes an expert to interpret what the number means. In the AHP the process is reversed with the expert judgment being made first as to dominance on pairs of elements, then a relative absolute scale of measurement is derived from the judgments.

MAKING THE DECISION WITH AN ABSOLUTE OR RATINGS MODEL

We will re-do the decision problem using the absolute or ratings method of the AHP in which the alternatives are rated one at a time assigning previously defined standards. Categories (intensities or standards) are established for each criterion and pairwise compared to determine their priorities. The alternatives are rated by picking the appropriate standard for each criterion. The score for a city is independent of the other cities' scores. This type of independent measuring is called absolute measurement; it is absolute measurement that one is using in applying a standard measure or scale such as a yardstick to measure distance.

The standards are prioritized for each criterion by making pairwise comparisons. For example, the standards for the criterion Job Opportunities are: Excellent, Above Average, Average, Below Average and Poor. Judgments are entered for such questions as: "How much more preferable is Excellent than Above Average for this criterion?" Each city is then rated by selecting the appropriate category for it for each criterion. The city's score is then computed by weighting the priority of the selected category by the priority of the criterion and summing for all the criteria.

The prioritized categories are essentially absolute scales, abstract yardsticks, which have been derived and are unique for each criterion. Judgment is still required to select the appropriate category under a criterion for a city, but the cities are no longer compared against each other. In absolute measurement, the cities are scored independently of each other. In relative measurement there is unavoidably dependence because a city's performance depends on what other cities it is being compared against. If they are all bad, it may shine. Figure 5-6 shows the structure of the ratings model.

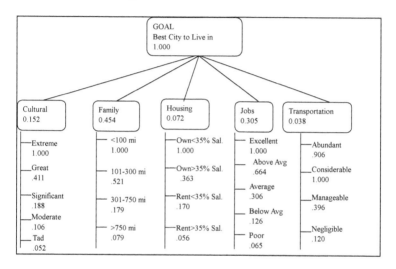

Figure 5-6 Absolute (ratings) mode for choosing a best city

Table 5-9 Pairwise judgments on rating categories for culture

	Extreme	Great	Signif-icant	Moder-ate	Tad	Derived Priorities	Idealized Priorities
Extreme	1	5	6	8	9	.569	1.000
Great	1/5	1	4	5	7	.234	.411
Significant	1/6	1/4	1	3	5	.107	.188
Moderate	1/8	1/5	1/3	1	4	.060	.106
Tad	1/9	1/7	1/5	1/4	1	.030	.052

Inconsistency = 0.112

As an example of obtaining the priorities for the ratings, we show the pairwise comparisons (for preference) of the ratings for the Culture criterion in Table 5-9. The rating categories for the other criteria were pairwise compared in the same way to obtain their priorities. The verbal ratings that were selected for the cities are given in. We caution that ratings priorities should be derived specifically for a particular criterion, and are not necessarily applicable to other criteria in the same problem. The priorities associated with the verbal ratings in Table 5-10 are shown in Table 5-11. The synthesis process to get the final priorities is the same multiply and add process described before.

Table 5-10 Verbal ratings of cities under each criterion

Alternatives	Cultural .195	Family .394	Housing .056	Jobs .325	Transport .030	Total Score	Priorities Normal.
Pittsburgh	Significant.	<100 mi	Own>35%	Avg	Manageable	.562	.294
Boston	Extreme	301-750 mi	Rent>35%	Above Avg	Abundant	.512	.267
Bethesda	Great	101-300 mi	Rent<35%	Excellent	Considerable	.650	.339
Santa Fe	Significant.	>750 mi	Own>35%	Avg	Negligible	.191	.100

Table 5-11 Verbal Ratings replaced by priorities

Alternatives	Cultural .195	Family .394	Housing .056	Jobs .325	Transport .030	Total Score	Final Priorities Normal.
Pittsburgh	0.188	1.000	0.363	0.306	0.396	.562	.294
Boston	1.000	0.179	0.056	0.664	0.906	.512	.267
Bethesda	0.411	0.521	0.170	1.000	1.000	.650	.339
Santa Fe	0.188	0.079	0.363	0.306	0.120	.191	.100

We see that by using ratings, instead of pairwise comparing the cities with respect to the criteria, again the best city is Pittsburgh. Note that the criteria have similar priorities and the same rank order, but the priorities are not exactly the same as they were in the relative measurement solution. The person making the decision chose to make the judgments for the criteria afresh for the ratings model and got slightly different answers, but the ratings mode can give a different ranking even if the priorities of the criteria remain the same.

An interesting effect of having different priorities for the criteria from those used in the first model is that the priority of family is smaller this time, 0.394 versus 0.454 in the first model. The diminished importance of family allowed the importance of Jobs to be greater and since Bethesda is much the best for jobs there is a new order for the cities: Bethesda, Pittsburgh, Boston, Santa Fe. This is an example of sensitivity analysis: the process of changing the priorities of the criteria to see the effect on the outcome.

RANKING 329 US CITIES BY RATING THEM ON NINE CRITERIA

Another example of an AHP ratings model is given here that ranked 329 cities in the United States by rating them with respect to nine criteria. There are two especially interesting aspects to this model:

- The ratings were established by breaking existing data on each criterion into ranges, prioritizing the ranges, then assigning the cities their appropriate category for each criterion, resulting in a database of city priorities on each criterion.

- An individual pairwise compares the criteria and applies his personalized criteria priorities to the database of city priorities resulting in a list of cities customized for the individual. Results are given here for six individuals who participated in the study in the form of a table listing the top 5 and bottom 5 cities for each.

The data for the cities for each criterion were based on the well-publicized Rand McNally *Places Rated Almanac* by R. Boyer and D. Savageau, 1985, in which they rated 329 American cities on 9 criteria and showed, among other things, that Pittsburgh is the most livable city in the United States.

In the Boyer and Savageau books, cities are assigned scores on each criterion, but the criteria themselves are treated equally. In the AHP model the criteria are prioritized. In this study each individual pairwise compared the criteria to determine the priorities which were then applied to the ratings of the cities on the criteria, resulting in a personalized ranking of the 329 cities.

From the *Places Rated Almanac* one can surmise a hierarchy of four levels. They are: the goal of selecting the most livable city, a set of nine criteria (climate, housing, healthcare, crime, transportation, education, arts, recreation, economics), a set of intensities or ratings under each criterion whose priorities are derived after making appropriate correspondence with scores they assign to each criterion based on several subcriteria, and finally 329 places or cities in the United States that are ranked according to the criteria. A big difference with the AHP model used here is that they did not assign weights to the criteria, considering them equal in importance.

We first took the following seven criterion ratings: excellent, very good, good, average, below average, poor, very poor and for each criterion that make a correspondence between ranges of scores and these ratings for each criterion in such a way as to approximate a symmetric distribution which starts at zero for the poorest rating and ends at a range for an excellent rating. The ratings under each criterion were then pairwise compared according to importance yielding numerical priorities. The score assigned to each city was associated with one of these ratings and translated to the corresponding priority. These priorities were then weighted by the importance of the criteria and added for that city to obtain its overall score. The following is a list of the criteria used by Boyer and Savageau.

1) Climate: very hot and very cold months, seasonal temperature variations, freezing days, zero degree days, and ninety degree days.
2) Housing: annual average utility bills, annual average property taxes, annual average mortgage payments.
3) Healthcare physicians per 100,000 residents, teaching hospitals, medical schools, cardiac rehabilitation centers, cancer treatment centers, hospices, insurance and hospital costs, fluoridation of drinking water, air pollution.
4) Crime: violent crime rate, property crime rate divided by ten.
5) Transportation: length of daily commute, public transportation, interstate highways, air service, passenger rail service.
6) Education: pupil/teacher ratio in the K-12 system, effort index in K-12, academic options in higher education.
7) Arts: museums, fine arts, public radio stations, public television, universities offering degrees in the arts,

symphony orchestras, theatres, opera companies, dance companies, public libraries.

8) Recreation: good restaurants, public golf courses, ten pin lanes, movie theatres, zoos, aquariums, family theme parks, sanctioned auto race tracks, pari-mutual betting attractions, major and minor league professional sports teams, NCAA division I football and basketball teams, miles of coastline and inland water, national forest and parks.

9) Economics: average household income adjusted for taxes and cost of living expenses, rate of income growth, rate of job expansion.

The weights of the criteria given below were provided by six people, labeled A to F, who made paired comparisons separately. We used these weights to obtain the final scores of the cities. Table 5-12 below shows their individual priorities, the eigenvectors (but not the paired comparison matrices leading to them) calculated from the six people's comparisons of the nine criteria.

A glance at the derived weights for the six people shows a striking difference of values and interests. Person A is greatly interested in Economics, Person B is more balanced with fairly similar priorities for all nine criteria, but showing a somewhat greater interest in Culture, person C is focused on Recreational Opportunities and so on. It is easy to see that no single ranking of cities will be universally appropriate.

Table 5-12 Priorities for criteria for six individuals A to F

	A	B	C	D	E	F
Climate	0.106	0.098	0.089	0.041	0.047	0.197
Housing	0.061	0.053	0.111	0.126	0.280	0.031
Healthcare	0.102	0.084	0.043	0.178	0.124	0.068
Crime	0.150	0.049	0.036	0.285	0.162	0.312
Transportation	0.026	0.051	0.070	0.030	0.068	0.139
Education	0.163	0.165	0.100	0.073	0.040	0.073
Arts	0.051	0.198	0.047	0.032	0.024	0.049
Recreation	0.034	0.150	0.339	0.047	0.023	0.097
Economics	0.308	0.152	0.165	0.187	0.233	0.034

Boyer and Savageau used a numerical scoring system they concocted for each criterion, coming up with a number for each city for each criterion, but the scores for the different criteria were not standard; the ranges varied widely as can be seen from Table 5-13.

We used 7 verbal ratings for each of the nine criteria, and derived priorities for them by pairwise comparing the verbal ratings for preference as shown in Table 5-13. We derived the priorities for the verbal ratings individually for each criterion.

Because of space limitations it is not possible for us to give all our pairwise comparisons here or include all the refinements we used to make our subjective assignment of ranges of scores to the verbal ratings. But for example, under Healthcare we not use the score from the Boyer and Savageau study, but instead used the number of Healthcare subcriteria a city satisfied. If a city satisfied 5 criteria we assigned it the priority we had derived for the 5-6 criteria category.

Table 5-13 Ratings for the criteria

	Climate		Housing		Healthcare	
	Score	Priority	Score	Priority	Score	Priority
Excellent	858-1000	0.357	0-6000	0.233	9	0.214
Very good	715-857	0.227	6001-7999	0.198	8	0.19
Good	572-714	0.161	8000-9999	0.154	7	0.168
Average	429-571	0.11	10000-11999	0.128	5-6	0.143
Below average	286-428	0.068	12000-13999	0.108	4	0.12
Poor	148-285	0.045	14000-15999	0.092	3	0.094
Very poor	1-147	0.031	16000	0.086	2	0.071

Table 6 (Continued)						
	Crime		Transportation		Education	
	Score	Priority	Score	Priority	Score	Priority
Excellent	300-614	0.331	7108-8625	0.237	3417-3700	0.354
Very good	615-928	0.195	6041-7107	0.208	3131-3416	0.24
Good	929-1242	0.14	5006-6040	0.174	2845-3130	0.159
Average	1243-1556	0.108	4001-5005	0.144	2559-2844	0.104
Below average	1557-1870	0.089	3018-4000	0.11	2273-2558	0.068
Poor	1871-2184	0.075	2000-3017	0.08	1987-2272	0.045
Very poor	2185-2500	0.061	1145-1999	0.048	1701-1986	0.031

Table 6 (Continued)						
	Arts		Recreation		Economics	
	Score	Priority	Score	Priority	Score	Priority
Excellent	17270 - 56745	0.353	4200-4800	0.355	9000-10000	0.391
Very good	11614 - 17269	0.239	3544-4199	0.241	8000-8999	0.245
Good	8058 - 11613	0.164	2881-3543	0.155	7000-7999	0.152
Average	6152 - 8057	0.103	2234-2880	0.104	6000-6999	0.094
Below average	4142 - 6151	0.067	1596-2233	0.068	5000-5999	0.058
Poor	2001-4141	0.043	946-1595	0.045	4000-4999	0.036
Very poor	52-2000	0.031	0-945	0.032	3000-3999	0.023

In our AHP model we assigned a priority to each city under each criterion using the appropriate priority for the Boyer and Savageau score from Table 5-13. This resulted in a table that was our database, which we are not showing here because of its size. For each individual we multiplied that individual's criterion priorities from Table 5-12 times the cities' priorities from our database and summed to obtain scores for all 329 cities for each person. In Table 5-14 we show the top 5 and bottom 5 cities for each person along with the cities' cores.

Table 5-14 Top and bottom 5 cities for the six individuals

	A			B	
1	Portsmouth, NH	20.272	1	San Francisco, CA	24.714
2	Nassau, NY	19.623	2	Los Angeles, CA	22.349
3	Lafayette, LA	19.422	3	Boston, MA	22.183
4	Midland, TX	19.385	4	Washington, DC	20.418
5	Boston, MA	18.059	5	Philadelphia, PA	20.295
325	Dothan, AL	8.461	325	Anniston, AL	7.146
326	Anniston, AL	8.351	326	Pine Bluff, AZ	7.015
327	Yuba City, CA	8.182	327	Benton Harbor, MI	6.990
328	Benton Harbor, MI	8.034	328	Yuba City, CA	6.913
329	Flint, MI	7.731	329	Dothan, AL	6.721

	C			D	
1	San Francisco, CA	24.478	1	Nassau, NY	21.189
2	Seattle, WA	20.965	2	Portsmouth, NH	20.845
3	Miami, FL	19.910	3	Burlington, VT	20.510
4	Los Angeles, CA	19.797	4	Albany, NY	19.756
5	Nassau, NY	19.176	5	Danbury, CT	18.575
325	Albany, GA	7.510	325	Yuba City, CA	10.138
326	Benton Harbor, MI	7.488	326	Stockton, CA	10.078
327	Pine Bluff, AR	7.426	327	New Bedford, MA	10.074
328	Dothan, AL	7.409	328	Jersey City, NJ	9.757
329	Yuba City, CA	7.165	329	Flint, MI	9.735

	E			F	
1	Lafayette, LA	19.381	1	San Francisco, CA	21.758
2	Portsmouth, NH	19.070	2	Nassau, NY	21.560
3	Midland, TX	18.961	3	Los Angeles, CA	20.896
4	Burlington, VT	17.840	4	Burlington, VT	20.621
5	Albany, NY	17.822	5	Albany, NY	20.228
325	Santa Barbara, CA	10.809	325	Panama City, FL	9.529
326	Santa Cruz, CA	10.690	326	Gainesville, TX	9.407
327	Reno, NV	10.677	327	Corpus Christi, TX	9.382
328	Jersey City, NJ	10.569	328	Dothan, AL	9.346
329	New Bedford, MA	10.539	329	Beaumont, TX	9.298

In another exercise we averaged the six sets of priorities to get a set of overall composite priorities for each criterion and re-calculated the scores for the cities. The result was this list of Best

Cities on Average: (1) Nassau, NY 19.69; (2) San Francisco, CA 19.64; (3) Los Angeles, CA 18.17; (4) Boston, MA 17.96; (5) Burlington, VT 17.63; (6) Portsmouth, NH 17.54; (7) Albany, NY 16.68; (8) Philadelphia, PA 16.39; (9) Seattle, WA 16.38; (10) Pittsburgh, PA 16.32; (11) Washington, DC 16.14; (12) Lafayette, LA 16.11; etc. The three lowest ranking cities are: (329) Flint, MI 8.98; (328) Yuba City, CA 8.99; (327) Benton Harbor, MI 9.11.

We believe averaged scores give the soundest ranking for the cities. It is well-known that averaging the outcomes of a decision process using several experts that obtained their results independently is a good way to obtain a group opinion. This is a statistical approach; the more people whose independent priorities for the cities are included, the better. We would have gotten more statistically valid results for our city ranking with 100 individuals. It is noteworthy that the AHP average outcome has given as the top cities the well-known commonly accepted most preferred cities, yet the best choices for each individual were relatively different.

The individuals had nothing to do with selecting the cities. They only judged the criteria. We had very little to do with judging the cities. We took their scores from the Rank McNally study and used the corresponding priorities we had derived for ranges of those scores. The outcome of this study is not only striking, but it is also objective as no one participating in the study – neither the researchers nor our 6 respondents – could particularly have anticipated what it was going to be. Although Pittsburgh, the Rand McNally number one city, was not first in any individual ranking, it came out as one of the 12 most livable cities in the average ranking. And look at Nassau, a bedroom community for

New York City that is far out on Long Island. It seems to have the best of everything.

In the next chapter we apply hierarchic thinking to choose among different types of cities by using separate hierarchies for benefits, opportunities, costs and risks, then combining the results into a single overall answer by using strategic criteria.

Chapter 6

Choosing the Best City for the Future

INTRODUCTION

In this chapter we describe various possibilities for the cities of the future, considering various constraints and the demands of society, environment and geography.

The need for a different kind of future cities arises because of the rapid growth in population that is causing a decline in urban living standards. In the United States itself, many people are moving to cities every day. Today cities are getting crowded and if the influx continues at the same rate, current cities will become unmanageable and unlivable.

More population means faster consumption of natural resources which eventually leads ecological imbalance. Already more than 80% of world's forests are gone. The food consumption has also doubled over the last fifty years and this has exerted pressure on the landscape through the use of artificial fertilizers. The use of artificial agents to boost agricultural productivity has significantly marred the flora and fauna leading to loss of huge amount of bio diversity.

Another problem with the increasing population and population migration to cities is the rise of congestion on the city roads. In United States a person in a year drives 7500 miles in 1600 hours with an average speed of 4.68 mph. To accommodate the population approximately 2000 trees are cut in a minute in the Amazon Forest alone.

On top of all that, with increasing wealth, the average house size has almost doubled since 1970 and this has further caused the decline of arable land and forests. To deal with the problem of rising population and congestion within the cities, we need to plan cities of the future that will be able to utilize the available resources in more efficient and cleaner manner. The future city project aims to delve into details of various future city models and aims to find out which model will be most suitable depending upon the strategic criteria that we have used to evaluate the various merits of the BOCR model.

THE FIRST MODEL – RANKING TODAY'S CITIES

The vision of what future cities will look like is based on emerging technology that is available now. This modern technology will have to be refined and downsized in many cases for production quality. One can look for nanotechnology to have taken over in many fields.

In today's world, we have topographically different kinds of cities; three dimensional skyscraper cities like Manhattan in New York (Figure 6-5), flat cities like Los Angeles, connected hill cities like Rome, water cities like Dubai , cold weather cities like those in Siberia, cities that combine two continents, like Istanbul which straddles two continents across the Bosphorus, mountain cities like La Paz, the highest city in the world (nearly 2 miles high), desert cities like Riyadh, underground cities like downtown Toronto's underground walkway path linking 28 kilometers of services and entertainment, and Moon and Mars kinds of cities like the fully enclosed Compact City. The following figures show the pictures of the metropolitan cities in the world that we used in this example.

For this example we selected seven well-known cities in the world, from among the numerous cities with millions of people, surrounded by metropolitan areas with complex structures and highly modern services and technologies, having characteristics that make them noticeably different. We ranked them in terms of various suitable criteria. Here is our city list with specific reasons why they were chosen as alternatives: Dubai (Figure 6-2) as a city on the water, Istanbul (Figure 6-3), as the only city which connects two continents, La Paz (Figure 6-4) as one of the highest capital cities in the world, New York for its three dimensions, Riyadh (Figure 6-6) as a city in the desert, Tokyo as one of the largest and most widely spread cities and finally Compact City (Figure 6-1).

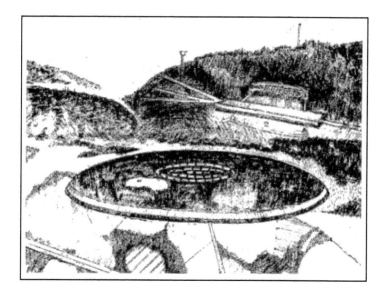

Figure 6-1 Compact City – the city of the future

Figure 6-2 Dubai - an example of a city in the water

Figure 6-3 Istanbul - a city on two continents

Figure 6-4 La Paz - the highest mountain capital city in the world

Figure 6-5 New York is a 3-dimensional city with sprouting skyscrapers

Figure 6-6 Riyadh in Saudi Arabia represents the flat desert city

Figure 6-7 Tokyo, the most populous city in the world, represents the greatest metropolises of the world

CRITERIA FOR RANKING TODAY'S CITIES FOR THEIR DESIRABILITY AS CITIES OF THE FUTURE

We structured our model in four parts to choose the best city from the seven cities shown in the pictures above: Benefits, Opportunities, Costs and Risks (BOCR). The BOCR nodes are called the merit nodes of the decision. Benefits and Costs apply to the present while Opportunities and Risks apply to the future. The criteria we identified include those used in the published literature related to city ranking (Cities Ranked and Rated by Bert Sperling and Peter Sander). While those authors used only criteria that are tangible, we have included intangible criteria that we measure in working out the exercise. Figure 6-8 shows the main structure of the model with the strategic criteria and the B, O, C, R.

Strategic criteria are the decision maker's criteria that are not directly related to a particular decision, but are higher level concerns that must be considered in every decision. Decisions are often driven more by one of the merits than the others. For example, a decision may be undertaken in large part because of the benefits it may offer. Strategic criteria are used to distinguish among and determine the priorities of the merits.

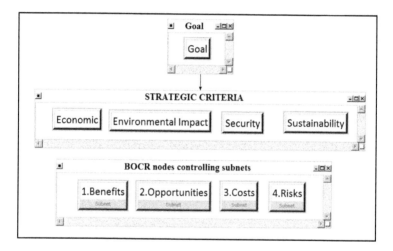

Figure 6-8 Top structure of the BOCR model

Figure 6-9 below represents the structure of the Benefits model. At the second level of the Benefits hierarchy are the criteria that we compare for importance with respect to their benefits and at the third level are the subcriteria we use to evaluate the candidate cities, the alternatives of the decision making process. Because of space limitations we abbreviate the subcriteria in the figures and list them in a table afterward along with the priorities for the cities in Benefits. Figure 6-10, Figure 6-11 and Figure 6-12 show the Opportunities, Costs and Risks structures respectively.

In each of these structures we pairwise compared the criteria with respect to the goal to determine their priorities, then pairwise compared the subcriteria with respect to their parent criterion to determine their priorities, then pairwise compared the cities with respect to each subcriterion. A weight and add process is used to determine the priorities of the alternatives which are shown at the bottom of each figure.

In the case of Benefits and Opportunities the pairwise question is always posed as which is more beneficial or affords more opportunity so that at the end of the process the highest priority city is the best.

For Costs and Risks the question posed is which is more costly or risky, so that in the end the worst alternative in the costs and risks model has the highest priority.

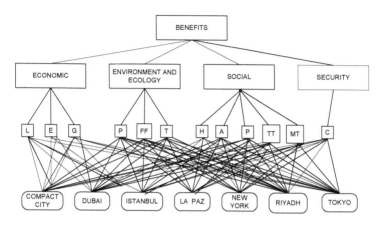

BENEFITS definitions of Criteria and Subcriteria labels				
	Label	Criteria	Label	Criteria
Economic	L	Living expenses	H	Housing
Economic	E	Energy consumption	A	Accessibility of health services
Economic	G	Per-capita income growth	P	Public services
Environment & Ecology	P	Pollution	TT	Time spent in traveling
Environment & Ecology	FF	Flora and fauna	MT	Metro areas
Environment & Ecology	T	Traffic	C	Crime rate
Security				

Figure 6-9 Benefits hierarchy for ranking kinds of cities

In the Benefits hierarchy, the best or most beneficial city has the highest priority. The best option is dominant in the pairwise comparisons. Benefits are things we can definitely say are good at the present time.

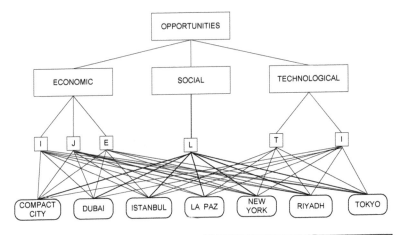

OPPORTUNITIES Criteria and Subcriteria					
Criteria	Label	Subcriteria	Criteria	Label	Subcriteria
Economic	I	Improving the budget	Technological	T	Better technological advances
	J	Job creation		I	Measures of innovation
	E	Expandability			
	L	Leisure time			
Social					

Figure 6-10 Opportunities hierarchy for ranking kinds of cities

In the Opportunities hierarchy, as in the Benefits hierarchy, the better city that offers more opportunities in a pairwise comparison has the highest priority. The final ranking in the Opportunities model has the city with the best ranked highest. By opportunities we mean potential benefits that might occur in the future.

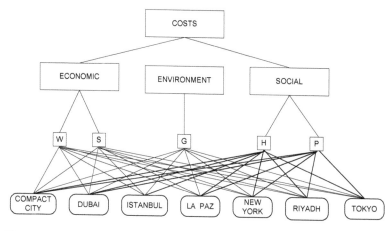

Table of COSTS Criteria and Subcriteria

Criteria	Label	Subcriteria	Criteria	Label	Subcriteria
Economic	W	Waste disposal	Environmental	G	Loosing green in favor of buildings
	S	Security cost			
Social	H	Heritage cost			
	P	Psychological cost due to traffic, air pollution and complexity			

Figure 6-11 Costs hierarchy for ranking kinds of cities

In the Costs hierarchy, judgments in the pairwise comparisons are made so the worse criteria and alternatives with respect to criteria get the higher priorites. Thus the highest priority city overall, under Costs, is the most costly or worst.

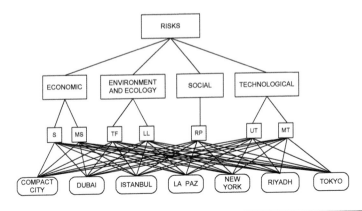

RISKS Criteria and Subcriteria					
Criteria	Label	Subcriteria	Criteria	Label	Subcriteria
Economic .449	S	Economic sustain- ability .75	Technological .288	UT	Uncertainty about technological feasibility .333
	MS	Risk in maintaining the public services .25		MT	Misuse of technology .666
Environ ment & Ecology	TF	Threat to flora and fauna .25	Social .126	RP	Population increase 1.0

Figure 6-12 Risks hierarchy and results for the riskiest city

In the Risks hierarchy, as in the Costs hierarchy, the worst or most Risky city has the highest priority. The worse option is dominant in the pairwise comparisons.

In Table 6-1 we give the priorities of the criteria and subcriteria obtained by making judgments in the BOCR hierarchies. We will show how the weights of the BOCR nodes were obtained in Table 6-3 using strategic criteria.

The numbers in the final column of Table 6-1, the overall priorities of the subcriteria in the BOCR hierarchies, are computed by multiplying the priority of the merit times the priority of the criterion times the priority of the subcriterion. For example in the first row Benefits (0.3) × Economic (0.44) × Living expenses (0.59) gives a Weighted Overall Priority for Living expenses of 0.077. The sum of the Weighted Overall Priorities in Table 6-1 is one.

Table 6-1 Priorities of the criteria in the BOCR hierarchies

BENEFITS (0.3)		Weighted Overall Priority
Criteria	Subcriteria	
Economic (0.44)	Living expenses (0.59)	0.077
	Energy consumption (0.25)	0.033
	Per-capita income growth (0.15)	0.019
Environment and ecology (0.14)	Pollution (0.33)	0.0138
	Traffic (0.52)	0.021
	Flora and fauna (0.14)	0.0058
Security (0.29)	Crime rate (1)	0.087
Social (0.13)	Housing (0.16)	0.006
	Accessibility of health services (0.23)	0.009
	Public services (0.175)	0.007
	Time spent in travelling (0.43)	0.016

OPPORTUNITIES (0.23)		Weighted Overall Priority
Criteria	Subcriteria	
Economic (0.43)	Improving the budget (0.32)	0.031
	Job creation (0.49)	0.048
	Expandability (0.19)	0.019
Social (0.15)	Leisure time (1)	0.036
Technological (0.42)	Better technological advances (0.67)	0.064
	Measures of innovation (0.33)	0.032

COSTS (0.27)		Weighted Overall Priority
Criteria	Subcriteria	
Economic (0.5)	Waste disposal (0.33)	0.044
	Security cost (0.66)	0.089
Social (0.25)	Heritage cost (0.5)	0.033
	Psychological cost (0.5)	0.033
Environment (0.25)	Loosing green (1)	0.067

RISKS (0.20)		Weighted Overall Priority
Criteria	Subcriteria	
Economic (0.45)	Economic sustainability (0.75)	0.068
	Risk in maintaining the public services(0.25)	0.022
Environment and ecology (0.14)	Threat to flora and fauna (0.25)	0.007
	Unacceptable losses of life (0.75)	0.021

Table 6-2 City rankings obtained from the BOCR hierarchies

Benefits

Here are the overall synthesized priorities for the alternatives. You synthesized from the network Subnet under 1.Benefits

Name	Graphic	Ideals	Normals
Compact City		1.000000	0.216340
Dubai		0.502743	0.108763
Istanbul		0.533595	0.115438
La Paz		0.431999	0.093459
New York		0.799029	0.172862
Riyadh		0.531382	0.114959
Tokyo		0.823604	0.178178

Opportunities

Here are the overall synthesized priorities for the alternatives. You synthesized from the network Subnet under 2.Opportunities

Name	Graphic	Ideals	Normals
Compact City		1.000000	0.254850
Dubai		0.401122	0.102226
Istanbul		0.534139	0.136125
La Paz		0.292494	0.074542
New York		0.668766	0.170435
Riyadh		0.290713	0.074088
Tokyo		0.736639	0.187733

Costs

Here are the overall synthesized priorities for the alternatives. You synthesized from the network Subnet under 3.Costs

Name	Graphic	Ideals	Normals
Compact City		1.000000	0.217129
Dubai		0.484172	0.105128
Istanbul		0.618186	0.134226
La Paz		0.384527	0.083492
New York		0.904339	0.196358
Riyadh		0.394728	0.085707
Tokyo		0.819607	0.177960

Risks

Here are the overall synthesized priorities for the alternatives. You synthesized from the network Subnet under 4.Risks

Name	Graphic	Ideals	Normals
Compact City		0.549072	0.115631
Dubai		0.539192	0.113550
Istanbul		0.651074	0.137112
La Paz		0.371215	0.078175
New York		1.000000	0.210594
Riyadh		0.638530	0.134470
Tokyo		0.999401	0.210467

In the overall priorities from the benefits and opportunities models, the best cities receive the highest priorities.

In the overall priorities from the costs and risks models, the worst cities receive the highest priorities. For example, with regard to Risks, New York (closely followed by Tokyo) was the most risky. We use two formulas to combine the results:, BO/CR, and bB+oO-cC-rR. There will be more about these formulas later, but as C and R are in the denominator of the first formula and are subtracted in the second formula, the higher the C and R priorities of an alternative, the more that alternative is penalized and the less likely to be the overall best choice.

The priorities for the verbal ratings shown in Table 6-3 were derived by pairwise comparing them for preference which yielded the following: High (1.0), Medium (0.55), and Low (0.30). The highest priority city for a merit is held in mind and rated for its impact on each of the strategic criteria across the row for that merit. For example, for Benefits, Compact City is the highest priority alternative so in the Benefits row one rates the impact (positive) that Compact City has on the strategic criteria: Economic (High), Environmental (Medium), Security (High) and Sustainability (High), as shown in the first row of Table 6-3. New York has the highest Risk, so in the Risks row one rates the impact (negative) that New York has on the strategic criteria.

Table 6-3 Rate the impact on the Strategic Criteria of the highest-priority alternative for each BOCR node

			Super Decisions Ratings			
	Priorities	Totals	Economic 0.424863	Environmental Impact 0.143784	Security 0.270066	Sustainability 0.161286
1.Benefits	0.300526	0.932613	High	Medium	High	High
2.Opportunities	0.227113	0.704792	Medium	High	High	Medium
3.Costs	0.266963	0.828457	High	Medium	High	Medium
4.Risks	0.205398	0.637405	Medium	Medium	High	Medium

Table 6-4 gives the overall outcome from combining the Benefits, Opportunities, Costs and Risks hierarchies using the weights of their priorities: b, o, c, and r, obtained from the ratings for impact in Table 6-3.

Table 6-4 gives the results using both the additive negative and multiplicative formulas. Compact City is the best overall choice using either formula. We interpret the formulas in this way: the additive (negative) formula gives the best long term choice while the multiplicative formula gives the best short term choice. This is analogous to the total and marginal investments which also employ additive and multiplicative formulas.

The two formulas do not necessarily always give the same ranking or the same best choice, though in this example they do. Compact City is the best choice and New York the worst using either formula, and even the ranks of the other cities are the same: La Paz is second, Dubai is the third and Tokyo comes in fourth.

Though the second place finish of La Paz is perhaps surprising, we see from the above table that it has the lowest priority of 0.37 under Risks, meaning it is by far the least risky. Perhaps its location, high in the mountains, in these days of global warming, makes it safe from possible submersion by the sea. La Paz is also the least costly city.

Table 6-4 Overall outcome using additive (negative) and multiplicative formulas

	Bene-fits	Oppor-tunities	Costs	Risks	Overall Outcome	
	(0.30)	(0.23)	(0.27)	(0.20)	Long term (additive)	Short Term (multip--licative)
					bB+oO-cC-rR	BO/CR
Compact City	1.00	1.00	1.00	0.54	1	1
Dubai	0.5	0.40	0.48	0.53	0.014	0.42
Istanbul	0.53	0.53	0.61	0.65	-0.11	0.38
La Paz	0.43	0.29	0.38	0.37	0.11	0.48
New York	0.79	0.66	0.90	1.00	-0.37	0.32
Riyadh	0.53	0.29	0.39	0.63	-0.07	0.33
Tokyo	0.82	0.73	0.81	0.99	-0.06	0.40

To further explore our outcome, we can perform sensitivity analysis. An example of the sensitivity graphs for Risk is shown In Figure 6-13.

In Figure 6-13 the priority of Risks is the point on the x-axis where the vertical line is located, and the y-values at which it intersects the colored lines in the graph are their priorities. It can be dragged back and forth. It is located at about 0.35 as shown here, and the priority of an alternative at x = 0.35 is read from the y-axis at the intersection of its colored line with the the dotted line. As Risks become more important in our model (the dotted line is dragged to the right), greater than a priority of about 0.35, La Paz, represented by the green line, becomes the best alternative. Note that as all lines fall below the x-axis after Risks = 0.35, all are bad alternatives, but LaPaz is the least bad of them.

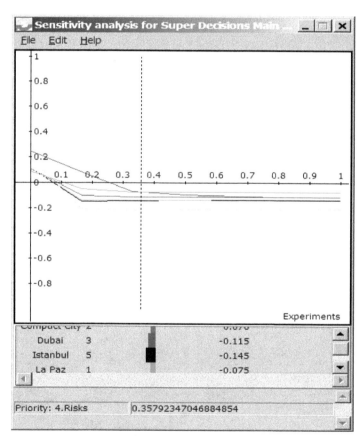

Figure 6-13 Sensitivity graph for Risks

THE SECOND MODEL - CHOOSING THE BEST CITY OF THE FUTURE

Now we turn to another way of looking at the decision problem of determining the best future city. There are four rather radically different kinds of cities that have been proposed as the ideal city of the future. We mentioned them in Chapter 3, and will now use the AHP decision process to rank them in order to choose the best one.

- Compact City
- Elevated City
- Green House City
- Water City

The goal of this model is to determine which of these proposed cities of the future is the most feasible and desirable. An Analytic Network Process (ANP) model of the BOCR type is used.

Figure 6-14 One vision of Compact City

The Analytic Network Process (ANP) is a generalization of the Analytic Hierarchy Process (AHP) that can take into account feedback and interdependence among the nodes. AHP decision structures are top-down from a goal, while ANP decision structures are networks that do not necessarily have a goal. The same pairwise comparison process is used to determine priorities.

The model for this example is a complex BOCR model with separate models used for analyzing benefits, opportunities, costs and risks. ANP network structures are used to evaluate the cities. There are many excellent references from which you can learn about the ANP, so we will not go into the details here but will give the priorities of the nodes and the results. See the books by Thomas Saaty listed in the References at the end of this book for more information about the Analytic Network Process. The *Principia Mathematica* book is perhaps the most comprehensive summary of the process. Another good resource is the series of *Encyclicon* books that contain hundreds of applications including many complex BOCR decision models.

Figure 6-15 shows the main model that is used to combine the results from the separate BOCR models. It contains the strategic criteria used to evaluate the importance of the BOCR nodes, the priorities of which are then used to combine results from the separate BOCR models to give the best overall answer. The BOCR priorities depend on the particular decision; sometimes Benefits are most important (and in this case the priority of Benefits has the highest weight as will be shown later). Or, Costs might be most important.

The priorities of the BOCR nodes are multiplied times their respective vectors of priorities of the cities and combined to determine the overall importance of the cities. The strategic criteria in Figure 6-15 are invariant higher-level concerns that must be considered in every decision and are used to evaluate the priorities of the BOCR nodes in the particular decision: Basic Necessities, Environment Friendly, Population Pressure, Social Life and Social Care.

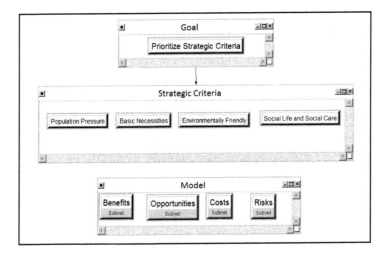

Figure 6-15 Top level of BOCR model to choose best future city

The screenshot in Figure 6-15 is from the *SuperDecisions* software that implements the AHP/ANP. A trial version of the software can be downloaded from www.superdecisions.com.

BENEFITS MODEL

The control criteria of the Benefits model are Economic, Environmental and Social, as shown in Figure 6-16. They are pairwise compared to prioritize them for their importance with respect to the Benefits the decision might bring. Each of the Benefits control criteria has a sub-network.

THE BENEFITS – ENVIRONMENTAL DECISION SUBNET

The Environmental control criterion under Benefits, with a priority of (0.594) the most important, "controls" the decision sub-network in which the alternatives are included, shown in Figure 6-18. We shall expand on the Benefits>Environmental decision subnet in detail here, but will give only the node names, priorities and results for the other bottom–level decision subnets.

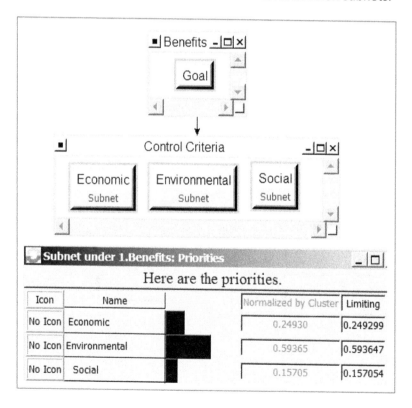

Figure 6-16 The Benefits control criteria and their priorities

Benefits>Environmental is a bottom level decision subnet, frequently modeled as an ANP network and not an AHP hierarchy. The criteria for environmental issues are in the Benefits>Environmental sub-model, grouped into three clusters: the Stakeholder cluster with the elements Air, Energy, Flora and Fauna, and Water; the Other cluster has the nodes Conservation, Enrichment, and Pollution; and the Alternatives cluster has the cities. The same cluster of cities must appear in every bottom level subnet and the outcome of the judgments, in the Benefits>Environmental subnet, for example, is a prioritization of the cities in that subnet.

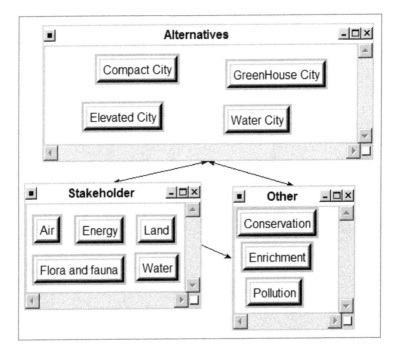

Figure 6-17 Decision subnet for the Benefits>Environmental control criterion

The lines going from one cluster to another, and sometimes both ways in this case, indicate there are links among the nodes, though there is no specific information in this view about what nodes are linked. Pairwise comparisons are made for nodes in one cluster with respect to the single node (the parent node of the comparison) they are linked from in another cluster.

The priorities of the Benefits>Environmental subnet nodes are shown in Figure 6-18: column 1 shows the nodes' values normalized by cluster; column 2 shows the nodes' overall priorities in the Benefits>Environmental subnet that sum to 1.0.

Subnet under 1.Benefits -> Environmental: Priorities			_ 日
Here are the priorities.			
Icon	Name	Normalized by Cluster	Limiting
No Icon	Compact City	0.32391	0.124582
No Icon	Elevated City	0.17822	0.068545
No Icon	GreenHouse City	0.35434	0.136286
No Icon	Water City	0.14352	0.055201
No Icon	Conservation	0.35790	0.117006
No Icon	Enrichment	0.12664	0.041401
No Icon	Pollution	0.51546	0.168513
No Icon	Air	0.09574	0.027617
No Icon	Energy	0.21332	0.061535
No Icon	Flora and fauna	0.22616	0.065239
No Icon	Land	0.26339	0.075979
No Icon	Water	0.20140	0.058097

Figure 6-18 Node priorities for the Benefits>Environmental sub-network and

The Benefits model has three control criteria: Environmental, Economic and Social and for each of these there is a decision subnet. The synthesis of results for the decision subnets are shown below.

BENEFITS – ENVIRONMENTAL SUBNET SYNTHESIS

The environmental benefits were measured on parameters such as reduced pollution, pressure on natural resources, energy conservation and the impact on flora and fauna. Figure 6-19 below shows the cities synthesized priorities in the environmental subnet. The synthesis shows that the Greenhouse City has the highest priority.

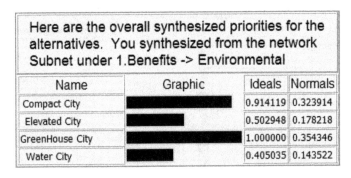

Figure 6-19 Synthesis of city priorities in the Benefits>Environmental subnet

Similarly there are subnets for Economic and Social. We will give the overall syntheses of priorities for them and not include screenshots.

The priorities of the cities in the Benefits>Environmental subnet also appear along with with the priorities of the other nodes in Column 1 of Figure 6-18. The cities are in every bottom level decision subnet.

BENEFITS – ECONOMIC SUBNET SYNTHESIS

The economic benefit has been measured on reduced expenses in living, maintenance and development of infrastructure, the cost for parking facility development and the transportation. The Figure 6-20 shown below gives the cities' priorities in the Benefits>Economic subnet. Elevated City has the highest priority.

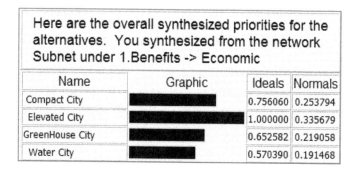

Here are the overall synthesized priorities for the alternatives. You synthesized from the network Subnet under 1.Benefits -> Economic

Name	Graphic	Ideals	Normals
Compact City		0.756060	0.253794
Elevated City		1.000000	0.335679
GreenHouse City		0.652582	0.219058
Water City		0.570390	0.191468

Figure 6-20 Synthesis of city priorities in Benefits>Economic subnet

BENEFITS – SOCIAL SUBNET SYNTHESIS

The Benefits>Social subnet measures the benefit of the future city in terms of time spent in traveling, housing needs of the increasing population, availability and quality of medical facilities, the quality of public services available and energy demand of the society for that city.

After synthesizing, the priorities of the alternative cities are as shown in Figure 6-21. For Social Benefits Compact City and GreenHouse City have close priorities with Greenhouse City coming out slightly ahead with a priority of 0.324.

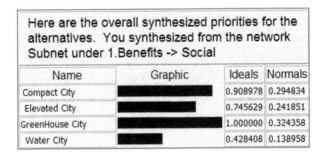

Figure 6-21 Cities' priorities in the Benefits>Social subnet

OVERALL BENEFITS SYNTHESIS

The nodes in the Benefits model and its three control criteria decision subnets are shown in Table 6-5 with their local priorities (priorities of nodes in the same cluster that sum to 1.0) and their global priorities.

The priorities of the cities in the control criteria subnets for Benefits are fairly different, so it is not apparent at a glance which city is best. As the priority of the Environmental control criterion node at 0.594 is much greater than that of Social at 0.157 and Economic at 0.249, the ranking under Environmental is going to count much more when the priorities of the four models are combined.

Table 6-5 Priorities of elements in the Benefits model

BENEFITS				
Criteria	Clusters	Elements	Local priorities	Global priorities
Social (0.157)	Administrative (0.094)	Security	0.780	0.012
		Public services	0.220	0.003
	Medical (0.257)	Availability	0.645	0.026
		Quality	0.355	0.014
	Quality of life (0.198)	Energy Needs	0.440	0.014
		Housing	0.401	0.012
		Time spent with family	0.159	0.005
	Government (0.451)	Policy executive	0.318	0.023
		Policy planning	0.182	0.013
		Public welfare department	0.500	0.035
Environmental (0.594)	Stakeholder (0.750)	Air	0.096	0.043
		Energy	0.213	0.095
		Flora and fauna	0.226	0.101
		Land	0.263	0.117
		Water	0.201	0.090
	Other (0.250)	Conservation	0.358	0.053
		Enrichment	0.127	0.019
		Pollution	0.515	0.076
Economic (0.249)	Industrialization (0.433)	Infrastructure development	0.554	0.060
		Jobs	0.446	0.048
	Administrative (0.165)	Maintenance	0.648	0.027
		Security	0.352	0.014
	Individual (0.094)	Income	0.414	0.010
		Living expenses	0.586	0.014
	Transportation (0.309)	Accident	0.124	0.010
		Gasoline	0.095	0.007
		Parking	0.260	0.020
		Road	0.288	0.022
		Vehicle	0.234	0.018

New synthesis for: Subnet under 1.Benefits

Here are the overall synthesized priorities for the alternatives. You synthesized from the network Subnet under 1.Benefits

Name	Graphic	Ideals	Normals
Compact City		0.956775	0.301119
Elevated City		0.728032	0.229128
GreenHouse City		1.000000	0.314723
Water City		0.492593	0.155030

Figure 6-22 Overall ranking of cities for Benefits

The final overall synthesis of city priorities in the Benefits model that combines the three subnets is shown in Figure 6-22 .

OPPORTUNITIES MODEL

The control criteria and their priorities from the Opportunities model are shown in Figure 6-23.

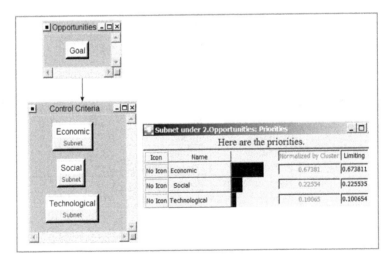

Figure 6-23 Control criteria in Opportunities model

Table 6-6 Priorities of all elements in the Opportunities model

OPPORTUNITIES				
Control Criteria	Clusters	Elements in Clusters	Local priorities	Global priorities
Economic (0.674)	Other (1.000)	Consulting	0.305	0.206
		Health Budget	0.112	0.076
		Job	0.480	0.324
		Security Budget	0.102	0.069
Social (0.226)	Other (1.000)	Crime Rate	0.234	0.053
		Custom and Tradition	0.038	0.008
		Health and Leisure	0.164	0.037
		Shared Community	0.148	0.033
		Social Harmony	0.216	0.049
		Work Life Balance	0.202	0.045
Technological (0.101)	Other (1.000)	Better forecasting	0.208	0.021
		Technical advances	0.602	0.061
		Technology sharing	0.190	0.019

The control criteria for Opportunities are Economic, Social, and Technological. The local and global priorities of all the nodes in the Opportunities model are shown Table 6-6. Local priorities sum to one for each control criterion. Global priorities sum to 1.0 overall.

OPPORTUNITIES – ECONOMIC SUBNET SYNTHESIS
The economic opportunities have been measured on the parameter such as opportunity in improving the budget for health and security, the opportunities for job creation for the increasing population. Figure 6-24 shows the synthesis results for the cities for the Opportunities>Economic subnet. Compact City has the highest priority.

Here are the overall synthesized priorities for the alternatives. You synthesized from the network Subnet under 2.Opportunities -> Economic					
Name	Graphic	Ideals	Normals	Raw	
Compact City		1.000000	0.373194	0.186597	
Elevated City		0.674019	0.251540	0.125770	
GreenHouse City		0.463604	0.173014	0.086507	
Water City		0.541946	0.202251	0.101126	

Figure 6-24 Priorities of the cities in the Opportunities>Economic subset

OPPORTUNITIES – SOCIAL SUBNET SYNTHESIS
The social opportunities offered by the future cities have been measured in terms of social harmony, work-life balance, reduced crime rate and opportunities for leisure time. Figure 6-25 below shows the synthesis for Opportunities>Social. The Elevated City has the highest priority of 0.418 (read from the Normals column in which the priorities sum to 1.0).

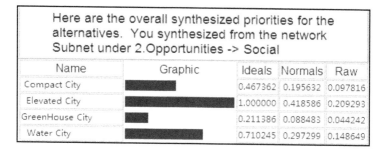

Here are the overall synthesized priorities for the alternatives. You synthesized from the network Subnet under 2.Opportunities -> Social				
Name	Graphic	Ideals	Normals	Raw
Compact City		0.467362	0.195632	0.097816
Elevated City		1.000000	0.418586	0.209293
GreenHouse City		0.211386	0.088483	0.044242
Water City		0.710245	0.297299	0.148649

Figure 6-25 Cities' priorities in the Opportunities>Social subnet

OPPORTUNITIES – TECHNOLOGICAL SUBNET SYNTHESIS

The technological opportunities offered by the future cities have been measured on parameters such as better technical advances in terms of technology sharing for improving the overall aspects of life. Figure 6-26 below gives the synthesis for the cities in the Opportunities>Technological subnet and the result shows that Water City has the highest priority.

Here are the overall synthesized priorities for the alternatives. You synthesized from the network Subnet under 2.Opportunities -> Technological				
Name	Graphic	Ideals	Normals	Raw
Compact City		0.138757	0.066114	0.033057
Elevated City		0.687251	0.327457	0.163729
GreenHouse City		0.272744	0.129955	0.064978
Water City		1.000000	0.476474	0.238237

Figure 6-26 Cities' priorities in the Opportunities>Technological subset

OVERALL OPPORTUNITIES SYNTHESIS

The overall best city with regard to opportunities, see Figure 6-27, is Compact City with a priority of 0.310. It is closely followed by the Elevated City with a priority of 0.293.

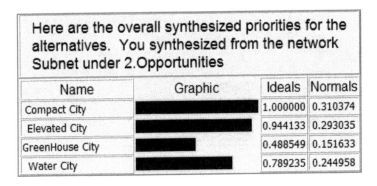

Name	Graphic	Ideals	Normals
Compact City		1.000000	0.310374
Elevated City		0.944133	0.293035
GreenHouse City		0.488549	0.151633
Water City		0.789235	0.244958

Here are the overall synthesized priorities for the alternatives. You synthesized from the network Subnet under 2.Opportunities

Figure 6-27 Overall ranking of cities for Opportunities

COSTS MODEL

The Costs model has control criteria of Environmental, Financial and Social costs. In the Costs and Risks models judgments are made as to the *most costly* and *most risky*, so that the worst alternative receives the highest priority.

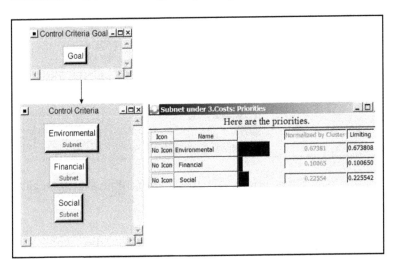

Figure 6-28 Priorities of the Costs control criteria

Figure 6-28 shows the control criteria for Costs and their priorities. Environmental Costs have the highest priority at 0.674, so it is believed that the environment is the concern that will be most costly.

The local priorities and global priorities of all the nodes in the Costs model are shown in Table 6-7. Remember that the higher the priorities of elements in the Costs model, the more costly they are, that is, less desirable.

Table 6-7 Priorities of all elements in the Costs model

COSTS				
Control Criterion	Clusters	Elements in Clusters	Local priorities	Global priorities
Social (0.226)	Other (1.000)	Acceptance	0.613	0.138
		Heritage	0.092	0.021
		Law and Order	0.000	0.000
		Social relations	0.295	0.067
Financial (0.101)	Administrative (0.200)	Legal	0.081	0.002
		Loss of productivity	0.597	0.012
		Process Implementation	0.322	0.006
		Demolition	0.107	0.009
	Other (0.800)	Development	0.211	0.017
		Loss of investment	0.000	0.000
		Maintenance	0.252	0.020
		Raw material	0.113	0.009

		Training	0.274	0.022
		Waste disposal	0.044	0.004
		Development	0.772	0.130
Environmental (0.674)	Other (0.250)	Waste management	0.228	0.038
		Climate	0.000	0.000
	Ecosystem (0.750)	Flora and fauna impact	1.000	0.505

COSTS – ENVIRONMENTAL SUBNET

The environmental costs have been measured in terms of waste management, development, flora and fauna impact and climate. Figure 6-29 below gives the synthesis of priorities for the cities in the environmental>costs subnet and the synthesis result shows that Water City has the highest cost at 0.382.

Here are the overall synthesized priorities for the alternatives. You synthesized from the network Subnet under 3.Costs -> Environmental

Name	Graphic	Ideals	Normals	Raw
Compact City		0.527859	0.201786	0.107997
Elevated City		0.612747	0.234236	0.125364
GreenHouse City		0.475329	0.181705	0.097249
Water City		1.000000	0.382273	0.204594

Figure 6-29 Priorities of cities in the Costs>Environmental subnet

COSTS – FINANCIAL SUBNET

The financial costs for the future cities have been measured in terms of development and maintenance costs for the city including waste disposal problems, raw material costs, loss in current investments that have already been made and the costs associated with the complexity of the process. Figure 6-30 below shows the synthesis for Costs>Financial with Water City having the maximum financial cost.

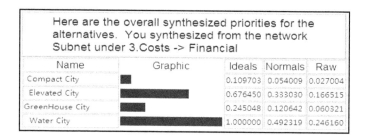

Name	Graphic	Ideals	Normals	Raw
Compact City		0.109703	0.054009	0.027004
Elevated City		0.676450	0.333030	0.166515
GreenHouse City		0.245048	0.120642	0.060321
Water City		1.000000	0.492319	0.246160

Here are the overall synthesized priorities for the alternatives. You synthesized from the network Subnet under 3.Costs -> Financial

Figure 6-30 Priorities of cities in the Costs>Financial subnet

COSTS – SOCIAL SUBNET

The social costs for the future cities have been measured in terms of heritage loss, acceptance cost (cost paid by individual for accepting the most acceptable alternative among the available) and lastly there may be some cost in maintaining law & order. Figure 6-31 below gives the Costs>Social synthesis of city priorities. Water City has the highest social costs with its priority of 0.523 being almost twice that of any other city.

Name	Graphic	Ideals	Normals	Raw
Compact City		0.108916	0.056995	0.028498
Elevated City		0.565323	0.295829	0.147915
GreenHouse City		0.236739	0.123884	0.061942
Water City		1.000000	0.523292	0.261646

Here are the overall synthesized priorities for the alternatives. You synthesized from the network Subnet under 3.Costs -> Social

Figure 6-31 Priorities of cities in Costs>Social subnet

OVERALL COSTS SYNTHESIS
The combined costs priorities for the cities are given in Figure 6-32.

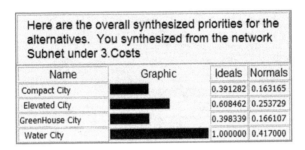

Figure 6-32 Overall ranking of cities for Costs

Water City, with a priority of 0.417, is much more costly than Elevated City at 0.254, probably due to the high environmental costs; the Environmental Costs control criterion has a priority of 0.674.

RISKS MODEL

In the Risks model in Figure 6-33, the four control criteria are shown: Financial, Environmental, Technological and Social Risks; and their priorities. In the Risks model just as in the Costs model the highest priority elements have the most risk, for example, Financial Risks, with a priority of 0.642, is considered to be the biggest risk.

It also shows the priorities of the alternatives under the Risks merit with Water Cities being the most risky as their priority is the highest under Risk. The local priorities and global priorities of all the nodes in the Risks model are shown in Table 6-8.

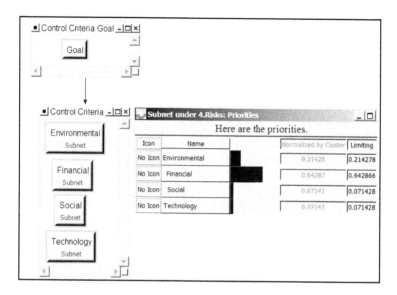

Figure 6-33 Risks control criteria and their priorities

Table 6-8 Priorities of elements in the Risks model

RISKS MODEL PRIORITIES				
Criteria	Clusters	Elements in Clusters	Local priorities	Global priorities
Social (0.071)	Others (1.000)	Acceptance risk	0.504	0.036
		Basic need support	0.320	0.023
		Crime rate	0.097	0.007
		Seclusion	0.078	0.006
Financial (0.643)	Stakeholder (0.250)	Government	0.508	0.082
		Public	0.492	0.079
	Acceptability (0.750)	Adaptability	0.409	0.197
		Affordability	0.236	0.114
		Self Freedom	0.067	0.033
		Self Sustainable	0.287	0.138
Environmental (0.214)	Other (1.000)	Disaster threats	0.631	0.135
		Flora and fauna	0.156	0.034
		Health	0.213	0.046

Technology (0.071)	Other (1.000)	Future technology changes	0.344	0.025
		Misuse	0.150	0.011
		Technical feasibilty	0.409	0.029
		Technology support	0.097	0.007

RISKS – ENVIRONMENTAL SUBNET SYNTHESIS

The environmental risks have been measured in terms of threat to flora & fauna, huge losses of life & property from natural calamities and the unknown risk to human health. Figure 6-34 shows the synthesis result. Water city has the highest environmental risk.

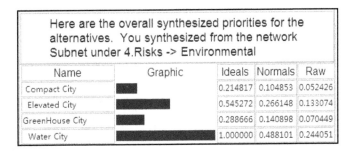

Here are the overall synthesized priorities for the alternatives. You synthesized from the network Subnet under 4.Risks -> Environmental

Name	Graphic	Ideals	Normals	Raw
Compact City		0.214817	0.104853	0.052426
Elevated City		0.545272	0.266148	0.133074
GreenHouse City		0.288666	0.140898	0.070449
Water City		1.000000	0.488101	0.244051

Figure 6-34 Overall synthesized priorities in Risks>Environmental

RISKS – FINANCIAL SUBNET SYNTHESIS

The financial risks for the future cities have been measured in terms of sustainability, adaptability and affordability. Moreover, there may be financial risks in maintain the public services. Figure 6-35 below shows the synthesis for financial risks with Water City having the highest financial risk.

Here are the overall synthesized priorities for the alternatives. You synthesized from the network Subnet under 4.Risks -> Financial				
Name	Graphic	Ideals	Normals	Raw
Compact City		0.532498	0.216403	0.036067
Elevated City		0.435437	0.176958	0.029493
GreenHouse City		0.492746	0.200248	0.033375
Water City		1.000000	0.406392	0.067732

Figure 6-35 Overall synthesized priorities in Risks>Financial subnet

RISKS – SOCIAL SUBNET SYNTHESIS
The social risks for the future cities have been measured in terms of crime rate, seclusion from near and dear ones and basic support from the society.

Here are the overall synthesized priorities for the alternatives. You synthesized from the network Subnet under 4.Risks -> Social				
Name	Graphic	Ideals	Normals	Raw
Compact City		0.996761	0.383032	0.191516
Elevated City		1.000000	0.384276	0.192138
GreenHouse City		0.257660	0.099013	0.049506
Water City		0.347873	0.133679	0.066840

Figure 6-36 Synthesized priorities of cities in Risks>Social

Figure 6-36 shows the risks>social subnet synthesis. Elevated City has the highest social risk though Compact City is a very close second.

RISKS – TECHNOLOGICAL SUBNET SYNTHESIS
The technological risks have been measured in terms of uncertainty about technological feasibility, misuse of technology, risk for dead-end towards further technological changes and the

increased support from technology for increasing population. Figure 6-37 shows the subnet for technological risks with Elevated city having the highest risk.

Here are the overall synthesized priorities for the alternatives. You synthesized from the network Subnet under 4.Risks -> Technology

Name	Graphic	Ideals	Normals	Raw
Compact City		0.174104	0.099436	0.049718
Elevated City		1.000000	0.571126	0.285563
GreenHouse City		0.173916	0.099328	0.049664
Water City		0.402908	0.230111	0.115056

Figure 6-37 Overall synthesized priorities under Risks>Technology

RATING THE BOCR UNDER THE STRATEGIC CRITERIA

The priorities of benefits, opportunities, costs and risks are determined by rating the highest priority in each model for its impact on the strategic criteria. The priorities of the strategic criteria: Population Pressure, Basic Necessities, Environment Friendly, and Social Life and Social Care are established by pairwise comparing them for importance. The priorities for the verbal ratings of High, Medium and Low, shown in Table 6-9 are derived through Pairwise comparisons. Each of the BOCR is then rated for how its top priority alternative impacts the strategic criteria: how good in the case of B and O and how bad in the case of C and R. The different priorities used for the BOCR make a difference only in the additive (negative) formula and this is the formula used for doing sensitivity on the results. In the multiplicative method the BOCR priorities do not apply and make no difference.

Table 6-9 Rating highest-priority alternatives to get priorities for Benefits, Opportunities, Costs and Risks

	Priorities	Totals	Population Pressure 0.136631	Basic Necessity 0.484620	Enviornmental Frier 0.074723	Social Life and Soc 0.304026
1.Benefits	0.174207	0.356152	Medium	Medium	High	Medium
2.Opportunities	0.325854	0.666184	High	Medium	High	High
3.Costs	0.357796	0.731488	High	High	Medium	Medium
4.Risks	0.142143	0.290600	Medium	Medium	Low	Medium

MULTIPLICATIVE FORMULA FOR BEST CITY

Figure 6-38 shows the result of synthesizing under benefits using the multiplicative formula BO/CR. This is the best option in the short-term. This synthesis shows that Compact City is the preferred short term alternative.

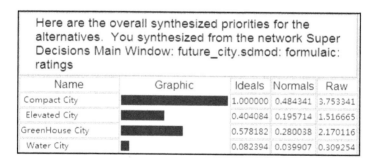

Figure 6-38 Overall synthesized priorities - multiplicative formula

ADDITIVE (NEGATIVE) SYNTHESIS

The additive (negative) method uses the priorities of the BOCR merits (b, o, c and r) obtained by rating them against the strategic criteria and B, O, C, and R, the priority vectors from the separate models. The formula used to combine them is bB + oO − cC − rR. Figure 6-39 below shows the additive-negative results with Compact City being the best long term alternative.

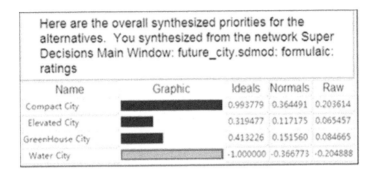

Figure 6-39 Overall synthesized priorities using the additive - negative formula

Table 6-10 Overall outcome gives the overall outcome obtained by combining the Benefits, Opportunities, Costs and Risks hierarchies using these formulas and priorities from Table 6-9: Long term (additive) bB+oO-cC-rR ; Short Term (multiplicative) BO / CR.

Table 6-10 Overall outcome

	Bene-fits (0.17)	Oppor-tunities (0.33)	Costs (0.36)	Risks (0.14)	Overall Outcome	
					Long term	Short Term
Compact City	0.957	1.000	0.391	0.518	1.000	1.000
Elevated City	0.728	0.944	0.608	0.592	0.320	0.400
Green-House City	1.000	0.489	0.398	0.450	0.410	0.580
Water City	0.493	0.789	1.000	1.000	-1.000	0.080

SENSITIVITY ANALYSIS

Sensitivity analysis is done to gauge the variance in the overall result due to a particular input parameter. We have done sensitivity analysis with respect to the weights of the benefits, opportunities, costs and risks as shown in the figures below.

In Figure 6-40 the sensitivity graph for benefits, on the left, shows that Compact City is clearly best up to about 0.60 on the x-axis for Benefits. When benefits become more important, Greenhouse City overtakes Compact City. In the graph on the right, the sensitivity graph for Opportunities, Compact City is best, but the second best, GreenHouse city is replaced by Elevated City after a priority on the x-axis of about 0.38.

In Figure 6-41 the sensitivity graphs for Costs, on the left, and Risks, on the right, shows that at a priority of more than about 0.50 for both, none of the cities is a good option as all are below the x-axis. However, if forced to choose one, Compact City is the best, followed by Elevated City.

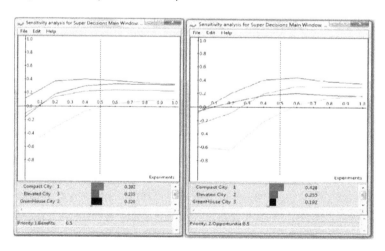

Figure 6-40 Benefits and Opportunities sensitivity graphs

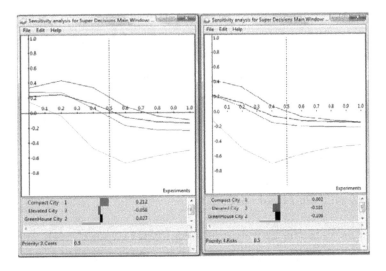

Figure 6-41 Costs and Risks sensitivity analysis

SUMMARY

Compact City was evaluated against three other futuristic cities that have been proposed: Elevated City, Greenhouse City and Water City using the approach of focusing on the factors of benefits, opportunities, costs and risks in four separate models and ranking the cities in each one. The importance of the four models was then determined using strategic criteria with their resulting priorities being: Benefits (0.17), Opportunities (0.33), Costs (0.36) and Risks (0.14), so the costs and opportunities were the main drivers in ranking the cities. Compact City was found to be best both for the short term and for the long term as it had the lowest cost and the highest opportunity, and thus it was the winner overall.

References

1) Alvin Toffler, Future Shock, Bantam Books (New York, 1971), page 475.

2) Achwal, Nilima. SMART: Global Urban Mobility Solutions. Ann Arbor, MI: GlobaLens, a division of The William Davidson Institute at the University of Michigan; 2010 Nov 19; Case 1-428-964.

3) Alusi, Annissa; Eccles, Robert G.; Edmondson, Amy C., and Zuzul, Tiona. Sustainable Cities: Oxymoron or The Shape of the Future? Cambridge, MA: Harvard Business School; 2011 Jan 7; Working Paper 11-062.

4) American Almanac 1970, "Statistical Abstract of U.S., Table 5 (Series D)," Grosset and Dunlap (New York, 1970), page 7.

5) Annez, Patricia Clarke and Linn, Johannes F. An Agenda for Research on Urbanization in Developing Countries: A Summary of Findings from a Scoping Exercise. Washington, DC: The World Bank; 2010 Nov; Policy Research Working Paper 5476 (WPS5476).

6) Annez, Patricia Clarke; Bertaud, Alain; Patel, Bimal, and Phatak, V. K. Working with the Market: Approach to Reducing Urban Slums in India. Washington, DC: The World Bank; 2010 Nov; Policy Research Working Paper 5475 (WPS5475).

7) Arifwidodo, S.D. and R. Perera, Quality of Life and Compact Development Policies in Bandung Indonesia, Applied Research in Quality of Life, Vol 6 (2), 159-179, 2010

8) Arku, Godwin. Rapidly Growing African Cities Need to Adopt Smart Growth Policies to Solve Urban Development Concerns. Urban Forum. 2009 Aug 1; 20(3):253-270; ISSN: 1015-3802.

9) Athey, Glenn; Nathan, Max; Webber, Chris, and Mahroum, Sami. Innovation and the city. Innovation: Management, Policy & Practice . 2008 Oct-2008 Dec 31; 10(2-3):156-169.

10) Basiago, A.D., The Search for Sustainable City in 20th Century Urban Planning, The Environmentalist, Vol. 16, no. 2, 135-155, 1996

11) Bay Area Rapid Transit District, "Fact Sheet II, Engineering Details of the General Bay Area Rapid Transit District," BART (Oakland, Calif.), July 19, 1971.

12) Boom Town. Newsweek, Sept. 14, 1970, page 68.

13) Boyer, R. and D. Savageau. Places Rated Almanac. Rand McNally, Chicago (1985).

14) Cadena, Andres; Remes, Jaana; Manyika, James; Dobbs, Richard; Roxburgh, Charles; Elstrodt, Heinz-Peter; Chaia, Alberto, and Restrepo, Alejandra. Building globally competitive cities: The key to Latin American growth. Washington, DC: McKinsey Global Institute; 2011.

15) Cai, Jianming and Sit, Victor. Measuring world city formation - The case of Shanghai: Globalization and Urban Development. Richardson, Harry W. and Bae, Chang-Hee Christine. Berlin: Springer Berlin Heidelberg; 2005; pp. 239-250. (Advances in Spatial Science.

16) Calthorpe, Peter. The Next American Metropolis: Ecology, Community and the American Dream, Princeton Architectural Press. Pp. 15-38, 1993.

17) Canfield, Christopher. Cerro Gordo: prototype symbiotic community, The Sustainability Project Designing for Sustainable Communities, Santa Barbara, April, 1994.

18) CEC, Green Paper on the Urban Environment, Brussels CEC, 1990.

19) Chacko, Elizabeth. From brain drain to brain gain: reverse migration to Bangalore and Hyderabad, India's globalizing high tech cities. GeoJournal ; 68:131-140.

20) Chen, S. and K. Karwan, Innovative cities in China: Lessons from Pudong New District, Zhangjiang High-tech Park and SMIC Village, Innovation: management, policy & practice, 10 (2-3), pp 247-256, October-December 2008

21) Clabby, Joe. IBM's Smarter City Initiative. Portland, Maine: Clabby Analytics; 2010 Jun; Research Report. . IBM's Smarter Systems Not Quite What We Expected. Portland, Maine: Clabby Analytics; 2010 Jun; Research Report.

22) Corbett, M. and Corbett, J. (1984). Energy and the Human Environment. College of Human Ecology Monograph Series, 103, 1-11, East Lansing: Michigan State University.

23) Couchman, Paul K.; McLoughlin, Ian, and Charles, David R. Lost in translation? Building science and innovation city strategies in Australia and the UK. Innovation: Management, Policy & Practice. 2008 Oct-2008 Dec 31; 10(2-3):211-223.

24) Dahaene, S., The Number Sense, How the Mind Creates Mathematics, Oxford University Press, 1997.

25) Dantzig, George B. and Saaty, Thomas L. Compact City: A Plan for a Liveable Urban Environment. San Francisco: W. H. Freeman and Company; 1973.

26) de Roo, Gert and Miller, Donald, eds. Compact Cities and Sustainable Urban Development: A Critical Assessment of Policies and Plans from an International Perspective. Aldershot, UK: Ashgate Publishing. ISBN: 0-7546-1537-5.

27) Devan, Janamitra; Negri, Stefano, and Woetzel, Jonathan R. Meeting the challenges of China's growing cities. McKinsey Quarterly. 2008(3):107-116.

28) Dirks, Susanne and Keeling, Mary. A vision of smarter cities: How cities can lead the way into a prosperous and sustainable future. Somers, NY: IBM Institute for Business Value; 2009; IBM Global Business Services Executive Report GBE03227-USEN-04.

29) Dirks, Susanne; Gurdgiev, Constantin, and Keeling, Mary. Smarter cities for smarter growth: How cities can optimize their systems for the talent-based economy. Somers, NY: IBM Institute for Business Value; 2010 May; IBM Global Business Services Executive Report GBE03348-USEN-00.

30) Dirks, Susanne; Keeling, Mary, and Dencik, Jacob. How Smart is your city? Helping cities measure progress. Somers, NY: IBM Institute for Business Value; 2009 Sep; IBM Global Business Services Executive Report GBE03248-USEN-00.

31) Dobbs, R. and J. Remes, Navigating Asia's New Urban Landscape, McKinsey Quarterly, McKinsey Global Institute, April 2011

32) Dobbs, Richard; Smit, Sven; Remes, Jaana; Manyika, James; Roxburgh, Charles, and Restrepo, Alejandra. Urban world: Mapping the economic power of cities. Washington, DC: McKinsey Global Institute; 2011 Mar.. Urban world: Mapping the economic power of cities - Executive Summary. Washington, DC: McKinsey Global Institute; 2011 Mar.

33) Donovan, John; Kilfeather, Eoin, and Buggy, Frances M. eGovernment for innovative cities of the next generation: The ICING Project. Innovation: Management, Policy & Practice. 2008; 10(2-3):293-302.

34) Doytsher, Yerach; Kelly, Paul; Khouri, Rafic; McLaren, Robin; Mueller, Hartmut, and Potsiou, Chryssy A. Rapid Urbanization

and Mega Cities: The Need for Spatial Information Management (Research study by FIG Commission 3). Copenhagen, Denmark: International Federation of Surveyors (FIG); 2010 Jan; FIG Publication No 48.

35) Ehrlich, Paul R. and Anne H., Population, Resources, Environment, Second Edition, Chapter 3, W.H. Freeman and Co, San Francisco, 1972.

36) Ewers, Michael. Migrants, markets and multinationals: competition among world cities for the highly skilled. GeoJournal. 2007 Feb 1; 68(2):119-130; ISSN: 0343-2521.

37) Fafchamps, Marcel and Shilpi, Forhad . Cities and Specialisation: Evidence from South Asia. The Economic Journal. 2005 Apr; 115:477-504.

38) FIG (International Federation of Surveyors) Commision 3, Rapid Urbanization and Megacities: The need for spatial Information Management, Publication no. 48, Jan. 2010.

39) Freudenberg, Nicholas. Intersectoral Approaches to Health Promotion in Cities: Health Promotion Evaluation Practices in the Americas 2009; 191-219; ISSN: 978-0-387-79733-5.

40) Geddes, Patrick. Cities in Evolution, Williams and Norgate, London,1915.

41) Girardet, Herebert. Closing the Circle, Town and Country Planning, 1990.

42) Girardet, Herbert. Cities: New Directions for Sustainable Urban Living, Gaia Books, London, 1992.

43) Goodman, Paul and Percival, Communitas, Vintage Press-Random House (New York, 1960), page 28.

44) Ha, O., D. Park, K. Lee, and J. Won, Evaluation Criteria for Road Networks in Residential Areas, KSCE Journal of Civil Engineering, Vol 15 (7), pp 1273-1284, 2011.

45) Heathcote, Edwin. Liveable v lovable . Financial Times. 2011 May 6.

46) Heinonen, Jukka and Junnila, Seppo. Implications of urban structure on carbon consumption in metropolitan areas. Environmental Research Letters. 2011; 6:1-9.

47) Hospers, Gert-Jan. Governance in innovative cities and the importance of branding. Innovation: Management, Policy & Practice. 2008; 10(2-3):224-234.

48) Howard, Ebenezer. Garden Cities of Tomorrow, Faber and Faber, London, 1902.

49) IBM. Planning and design for smarter cities. Somers, NY: IBM Corporation, Software Group; 2010; RAB14038-USEN-00.

50) India's urban awakening: Building inclusive cities, sustaining economic growth. Washington, DC: McKinsey Global Institute; 2010.

51) Introduction: High-Rise Living in Asian Cities [Chapter 1]. in : Yuen, Belinda and Yeh, Anthony G. O., eds. High-Rise Living in Asian Cities. New York: Springer Science+Business Media; 2011; pp. 1-8.

52) Jacobs Jane, The Death and Life of Great American Cities, Random House (New York, 1961).

53) Jenks, Mike and Burgess, Rod. Compact cities: Sustainable urban forms for developing countries. London : Spon; 2000.

54) Johnson, Bjorn. Cities, systems of innovation and economic development. Innovation: Management, Policy & Practice. 2008; 10(2-3):146-155.

55) Jonathan W. et.al, Preparing China's Urban Billion, McKinsey Global Institute, March 2009

56) Kaya, Travis. Professor's iPhone App Gets Users Off the Beaten Path. The Chronicle of Higher Education. 2010 Nov 22.

57) Keller, Ingrid M. and Kalache, Alex. Promoting healthy aging in cities: The Healthy Cities project in Europe. Journal of Cross-Cultural Gerontology. 1997 Dec 1; 12(4):287-298; ISSN: 0169-3816.

58) Kennedy, Daniel P. and Adolphs, Ralph. Stress and the city . Nature. 2011 Jun 23; 474 :452-453.

59) Lee, G.K.L. and E.H.W. Chan, The Analytic Hierarchy Process (AHP) Approach for Assessment of Urban Renewal Proposals, Soc Indic Res 89: 155-168, 2008

60) Lee, J, H. Je, and J. Byun, Wellbeing Index of Super Tall Residential Buildings in Korea, Building and Environment, Vol. 46 (5), pp 1184-1194, May 2011

61) Lee, Sang-Ho; Yigitcanlar, Tan; Han, Jung-Hoon, and Leem, Youn-Taik. Ubiquitous urban infrastructure: Infrastructure planning and development in Korea. Innovation: Management, Policy & Practice. 2008; 10(2-3):282-292.

62) Leon, Nick. Attract and connect: The 22@Barcelona innovation district and the internationalisation of Barcelona business. Innovation: Management, Policy & Practice. 2008; 10(2-3):235-246.

63) Levy, J.K. and K. Taji, Group Decision Support for Hazards Planning and Emergency Management: A Group Analytic Network Process (GANP) approach, Mathematical and Computer Modelling 46, 906-917, 2007

64) Levy, J.K., Multiple Criteria Decision Making and Decision Support Systems for Flood Risk Management, Stoch. Environ Res. Risk Assess, 19: 438-447, 2005

65) Li, Wei and Teixeira, Carlos. Introduction: immigrants and transnational experiences in world cities. GeoJournal. 2007 Feb 1; 68(2):93-102; ISSN: 0343-2521.

66) Lombardi, P., S. Giordano, A. Caragliu, C.D. Bo, M. Deakin, P. Nijkamp, K. Kourtit, An Advanced Triple-helix Network Model for Smart Cities Performance, Research Memorandum 2011-45, Faculty of Economics and Business Administration, Vrije Universiteit, Amsterdam

67) Lyle, John T. Designing green infrastructure, The Sustainability Project, Designing for Sustainable Communities, Santa Barbara: AIA,1994.

68) Maffei, Stefano; Arquilla, Venanzio, and Bianchini, Massimo. Designing a New Generation of Services for Urban Contexts. a New Educational Approach to Service Design Development. Proceedings of EDULEARN10 Conference; Barcelona, Spain. 843-850.

69) Marceau, Jane. Introduction: Innovation in the city and innovative cities. Innovation: Management, Policy & Practice. 2008; 10(2-3):136-145.

70) Martin, Ron and Simmie, James. Path dependence and local innovation systems in city-regions. Innovation: Management, Policy & Practice. 2008 Oct-2008 Dec 31; 10 (2-3):183-196.

71) McCarthy, Florence and Vickers, Margaret. Digital natives, dropouts and refugees: Educational challenges for innovative cities. Innovation: Management, Policy & Practice. 2008; 10(2-3):257-268.

72) McDonald, Margot. Los Osos, California: a proposal for a sustainable community within a sustainable watershed, 1994.

73) McDonough, William. The Hannover Principle, William McDonough, New York, 1992.

74) McHarg, Ian. Design with Nature, Philadelphia, Natural History Press, pp. 19-53,1969.

75) Meltzer, Rachel and Schuetz, Jenny. Bodegas or Bagel Shops? Neighborhood Differences in Retail & Household Services. 2010 Oct 26.

76) Mingardo, Giuliano. Cities and innovative urban transport policies. Innovation: Management, Policy & Practice. 2008; 10(2-3):269-281.

77) Mohr, Vivian and Garnsey, Elizabeth. Exploring the Constituents of Growth in a Technology Cluster: Evidence from Cambridge, UK. Cambridge, UK: Centre for Technology Management, Institute for Manufacturing, University of Cambridge; 2010 Sep; Centre for Technology Management Working Paper Series No: 2010/01.

78) Mollison, Bill. Permaculture. Tasmania: Kagari Books, 1978.

79) Morrison, Nicola. The compact city: Theory versus practice⬚⬚⬚The case of Cambridge. Journal of Housing and the Built Environment. 1998 Jun 1; 13(2):157-179; ISSN: 1566-4910.

80) Mucciolo, B., The Buildup of Safe Cities – An Emerging Market for Defence and Security Players, Frost & Sullivan, June 2011

81) Mukherji, Nivedita and Silberman, Jonathan. Absorptive Capacity, Knowledge Flows and Innovation in US Metropolitan Areas. 2011 Jul 18.

82) Mumford, Lewis. The Culture of Cities, Harcourt, Brace and Co. (New York, 1938)

83) Mumford, Lewis. The City in History, Harcourt, Brace and World, Inc., New York, 1961.

84) Mumford, Lewis. The Highway and the City, Secker and Warburg, London, 1963, and Harcourt Brace Jovanovich, Inc., New York, 1963.

85) Murata, Kiyoshi and Orito, Yohko. Japanese Risk Society: Trying to Create Complete Security and Safety Using Information and Communication Technology. SIGCAS Computers and Society. 2010 Jun; 40(2):38-49.

86) Nash, Robert. Island Civilisation, Wild Earth, Winter, 1991.

87) Nechyba, T. and R. Walsh, Urban Sprawl, Journal of of Economic Perspectives, Fall 2004

88) Neiburger, Morris, quoted in San Francisco Chronicle, August 9, 1965, page 12.

89) Neiman, Andrea and Hall, Mary. Urbanization and Health Promotion: Global Perspectives on Health Promotion Effectiveness [Chap. 13]. In. Global Perspectives on Health Promotion EffectivenessMcQueen, David V. and Jones, Catherine M., eds. New York: Springer New York; 2007; pp. 201-224.

90) Pearson, Nancy; Lesser, Eric, and Sapp, Joel (IBM Institute for Business Value). A new way of working: Insights from global leaders. Somers, NY: IBM; 2010; IBM Global Business Services Executive Report GBE03295-USEN-00.

91) Pichardo-Muñiz, Arlette. The Role of Diseconomies of Transportation and Public Safety Problems in the Measurement of Urban Quality of Life. Applied Research in Quality of Life.

92) Pinnegar, Simon; Marceau, Jane, and Randolph, Bill. Innovation for a carbon constrained city: Challenges for the built environment industry. Innovation: Management, Policy & Practice. 2008; 10(2-3):303-315.

93) Preparing for China's Urban Billion: Executive Summary. Washington, DC: McKinsey Global Institute; 2009.

94) Promoting healthy aging in cities: The Healthy Cities project in Europe. Journal of Cross-Cultural Gerontology. 1997 Dec 1; 12(4):287-298; ISSN: 0169-3816.

95) Rouse, James W., "Cities that Work for Man – Victory Ahead," address at University of Puerto Rico symposium on "The City of the Future," Oct. 18, 1967.

96) Saaty, Thomas L. Axiomatic Foundation of the Analytic Hierarchy Process. Management Science. 1986; 32(7):841-855.

97) Saaty, Thomas L., Principia Mathematica Decernendi: Mathematical Principles of Decision Making, RWS Publications, 4922 Ellsworth Avenue, Pittsburgh, PA 15213, 2010.

98) Saaty, Thomas L. and Kirti Peniwati, Group Decision Making: Drawing out and Reconciling Differences, RWS Publications, 4922 Ellsworth Avenue, Pittsburgh, PA 15213, 2008.

99) Saaty, Thomas L. and L.G. Vargas, Decision Making with the Analytic Network Process: Economic, Political, Social and Technological Applications with benefits, Opportunities, Costs and Risks, 2006, Springer's International Series.

100) Saaty, Thomas L., Theory and Applications of the Analytic Network Process, RWS Publications, 4922 Ellsworth Avenue, Pittsburgh, PA 15213, 2005.

101) Saaty, Thomas L., Fundamentals of Decision Making with the Analytic Hierarchy Process, paperback, RWS Publications, 4922 Ellsworth Avenue, Pittsburgh, PA 15213-2807, original edition 1994, revised 2000.

102) Saaty, Thomas L., Decision Making for Leaders; The Analytical Hierarchy Process for Decisions in a Complex World, Wadsworth, Belmont, CA, 1982. Translated to French, Indonesian, Spanish, Korean, Arabic, Persian, Thai. Latest revised version, RWS Publications, Pittsburgh, 2000.

103) Sankhe, Shirish; Vittal, Ireena; Dobbs, Richard; Mohan, Ajit; Gulati, Ankur; Ablett, Jonathan; Gupta, Shishir; Kim, Alex; Paul, Sudipto; Sanghvi, Aditya, and Sethy, Gurpreet. India's urban awakening: Building inclusive cities, sustaining economic growth - Executive Summary. Washington, DC: McKinsey Global Institute; 2010.

104) Scientific American, Cities, Vol. 213, No. 3, September 1965 (for a good survey of the evolution of our cities, their current problems, and future prospects see this special issue)

105) Sipahi, S., The Analytic Hierarchy Process and Analytic Network Process: An overview of applications, Management Decision, Vol. 48 (5), 2010

106) Sirgy, M.J., Societal QOL is More than the Sum of QOL of Individuals: The Whole is Greater than the Sum of the Parts, Applied Research Quality Life, The International Society for Quality-of-Life Studies (ISQOLS), 2010.

107) Stanford Environmental Law Society, San Jose: Sprawling City, Stanford University Press (Stanford, Calif., 1971), 109 pages. Also, Editors of Fortune magazine, The Exploding Metropolis, Doubleday (Garden City, N.Y., 1958), 177 pages.

108) Stanford Research Institute, Future Urban Transportation Systems, Final Report, I, Stanford Research Institute (Menlo Park, Calif., March 1968), pages 51-63.

109) SURF-ARUP Framework for Urban Infrastructural Development. The Centre for Sustainable Urban and Regional Futures. University of Salford. Manchester, UK.

110) Takano, Takehito. Health and environment in the context of urbanization. Environmental Health and Preventive Medicine. 2007 Mar 1; 12(2):51-55; ISSN: 1342-078X.

111) Tao, C.C and C.C. Hung, A Comparative Approach of the Quantitative Models for Sustainabe Transportation, Journal of the Eastern Asia Society for Transportation Studies, Vol 5, Oct. 2003

112) The Greater IBM Connection. News: 100 Cities, $50 Million: IBM Pledge to Improve 100 Cities Across the Globe in the Smarter Cities Challenge [Web Page]. 2010 Nov 9. Available at: https://www.ibmconnection.com/news/1305.

113) Tran, L.T., C.G. Knight, R.V. O'Neill, E.R. Smith, Integrated Environmental Assessment of the Mid-Atlantic Region with Analytical Network Process, Environmental Monitoring and Assessment 94: 263-277, 2004

114) U.S. Department of Transportation, Economic Consequences of Automobile Accident Injuries, U.S. Government Printing Office (Washington, D.C., 1970), 1.17:AO 2, 1970. 2 vols. and supplement.

115) Ushakov, I., Histories of Scientific Insights, Personally Published Book, 2007.

116) Van Assche, Jo; Block, Thomas, and Reynaert, Herwig. Can Community Indicators Live Up to Their Expectations? The Case of the Flemish City Monitor for Livable and Sustainable Urban Development. Applied Research in Quality of Life; 5:341-352.

117) Van Geenhuizen, Marina and Nijkamp, Peter. Place-bound versus footloose firms: wiring metropolitan areas in a policy context. The Annals of Regional Science. 2009 Dec 1; 43(4):879-896; ISSN: 0570-1864.

118) Van Geenhuizen, Marina. Modelling dynamics of knowledge networks and local connectedness: a case study of urban high-tech companies in The Netherlands. The Annals of Regional Science. 2007 Dec 1; 41(4):813-833; ISSN: 0570-1864.

119) Van Winden, Willem. Urban governance in the knowledge-based economy: Challenges for different city types. Innovation: Management, Policy & Practice. 2008 Oct-2008 Dec 31; 10(2-3):197-210.

120) Walls, Jacqueline. American Cities of the Future 2011/12 Winners. FDi Magazine . 2011 Apr-2011 May 31:28-34.

121) Washington Metropolitan Area Transit Authority, "Metro News Release," Wash. Metro. Area Transit Auth. (950 L'Enfant Plaza South, S.W., Washington, D.C.), December 31, 1970.

122) Wladawsky-Berger, Irving. What are the Key Qualities of a Great City?

123) Woetzel, Jonathan; Mendonca, Lenny; Devan, Janamitra; Negri, Stefano; Hu, Yangmei; Jordan, Luke; Li, Xiujun; Maasry, Alexander; Tsen, Geoff, and Yu, Flora. Preparing for China's urban billion. Washington, DC: McKinsey Global Institute; 2009.

124) Wolfe, David A. and Bramwell, Allison. Innovation, creativity and governance: Social dynamics of economic performance in city-regions. Innovation: Management, Policy & Practice. 2008 Oct-2008 Dec 31; 10(2-3):170-182.

125) Wong, Tai-Chee and Yuen, Belinda. Understanding the Origins and Evolution of Eco-city Development: An Introduction [Chapter 1]. in : Wong, Tai-Chee and Yuen, Belinda, eds. Eco-city Planning. Springer Science+Business Media: New York; 2011; pp. 1-14. ISSN: 978-94-007-0383-4.

126) World Business Council for Sustainable Development. A World of Sustainable Cities: Urban challenges & opportunities. World Business Council for Sustainable Development; Geneva, Switzerland UII flyer.pdf.

127) Wright, F.L. Broadacre City: a new community plan. The Architectural Record, Apr., pp.243-54, 1935.

128) Yeh, Anthony G. O. and Yuen, Belinda. Introduction: High-Rise Living in Asian Cities2011; 1-8; ISSN: 978-90-481-9738-5.

129) Yen, H.H., An Evaluation of Leisure Agriculture Policy in Taiwan Utilizing the Analytic Hierarchy Process (AHP), a dissertation submitted to Michigan State University, Department of Park, Recreation, and Tourism Resources, 2005

130) Yuen, Belinda. Liveability of Tall Residential Buildings: High-Rise Living in Asian Cities2011; 129-147; ISSN: 978-90-481-9738-5.

Appendix
Table of the World's Largest Cities

The Principal Agglomerations of the World with statistics and charts, maps, diagrams and tables were assembled by Thomas Brinkhoff. The following list of cities was taken from his work *The Principal Agglomerations of the World*, all agglomerations of the world with a population of 1 million inhabitants or more, from http://www.citypopulation.de on the reference date July 2012.

Rank	Name	English Name	Country	Population
1	Tōkyō	Tokyo *incl. Yokohama, Kawasaki, Saitama*	Japan	34,500,000
2	Guangzhou	Canton *Northern Pearl River Delta incl. Dongguan, Foshan, Jiangmen, Zhongshan*	China	25,900,000
3	Shanghai	Shanghai *incl. Suzhou*	China	25,500,000
4	Jakarta	Jakarta *incl. Bekasi, Bogor, Depok, Tangerang, Tangerang Selatan*	Indonesia	25,400,000
4	Seoul	Seoul *incl. Bucheon, Goyang, Incheon, Seongnam, Suweon*	S. Korea	25,400,000
6	Ciudad de México	Mexico City *incl. Nezahual-cóyotl, Ecatepec, Naucalpan*	Mexico	23,300,000
9	New York	NY *incl. Bridgeport, Newark, New Haven*	USA	21,500,000

11	São Paulo	São Paulo *incl. Guarulhos*	Brazil	21,200,000
12	Mumbai	Bombay *incl. Bhiwandi, Kalyan, Thane, Ulhasnagar, Vasai-Virar*	India	20,900,000
13	Los Angeles	Los Angeles *incl. Anaheim, Riverside*	USA	17,000,000
14	Ōsaka	Osaka *incl. Kobe, Kyoto*	Japan	16,800,000
15	Beijing	Beijing	China	16,500,000
16	Moskva	Moscow	Russia	16,200,000
17	Al-Qāhirah	Cairo *incl. Al-Jizah, Hulwan, Shubra al-Khaymah*	Egypt	15,800,000
18	Kolkata	Calcutta *incl. Haora*	India	15,700,000
19	Buenos Aires	Buenos Aires *incl. San Justo, La Plata*	Argentina	14,300,000
20	Dhaka	Dacca	Bangladesh	14,100,000
21	Krung Thep	Bangkok	Thailand	14,000,000
22	Tehrān	Tehran *incl. Karaj*	Iran	13,600,000
23	İstanbul	Istanbul	Turkey	13,500,000
24	Lagos	Lagos	Nigeria	12,800,000
25	Rio de Janeiro	Rio de Janeiro *incl. Nova Iguaçu, São Gonçalo*	Brazil	12,700,000
27	Paris	Paris	France	10,600,000
28	Shenzhen	Shenzhen	China	9,900,000
28	Tianjin	Tientsin	China	9,900,000
30	Chicago	Chicago	USA	9,750,000
31	Kinshasa	Kinshasa	Congo (D. Rep.)	9,600,000
32	Lima	Lima	Peru	9,450,000
33	Chennai	Madras	India	9,300,000
34	Bengaluru	Bangalore	India	9,250,000
35	Lahore	Lahore	Pakistan	9,200,000
36	Wuhan	Wuhan	China	9,150,000
37	Bogotá	Bogotá	Colombia	9,000,000
38	Taipei	Taipei *incl. Taoyuan & most parts of Xinbei / New Taipei*	Taiwan (R.. of China)	8,900,000
39	Nagoya	Nagoya	Japan	8,400,000

40	Hyderābād	Hyderabad	India	8,300,000	
41	Johannesburg	Johannesburg *incl. Soweto, East Rand, West Rand*	South Africa	8,000,000	
41	Washington	Washington *incl. Baltimore*	USA	8,000,000	
43	Thành Phố Hồ Chí Minh	Saigon *incl. Biên Hòa*	Vietnam	7,900,000	
44	Philadelphia	Philadelphia *incl. Allentown, Trenton*	USA	7,250,000	
45	Boston	Boston *incl. Providence*	USA	7,200,000	
46	San Francisco	San Francisco *incl. Concord, Oakland, San Jose, Santa Rosa*	USA	7,150,000	
46	Shenyang	Shenyang *incl. Fushun*	China	7,150,000	
48	Hong Kong	Hong Kong *incl. Kowloon, Victoria*	China	7,100,000	
49	Ahmadābād	Ahmedabad	India	6,800,000	
50	Madrid	Madrid	Spain	6,650,000	
51	Singapore	Singapore *incl. Johor Bahru (Malaysia)*	Singapore	6,550,000	
52	Kuala Lumpur	Kuala Lumpur *incl. Klang*	Malaysia	6,500,000	
53	Baghdād	Baghdad	Iraq	6,300,000	
53	Chengdu	Chengtu	China	6,300,000	
55	Chongqing	Chungking	China	6,250,000	
55	Dallas	Dallas *incl. Fort Worth*	USA	6,250,000	
57	Santiago	Santiago	Chile	6,100,000	
58	Xi'an	Sian *incl. Xianyang*	China	6,050,000	
59	Ar-Riyād	Riyadh	Saudi Arabia	5,850,000	
59	Belo Horizonte	Belo Horizonte	Brazil	5,850,000	
59	Luanda	Luanda	Angola	5,850,000	
59	Toronto	Toronto	Canada	5,850,000	
63	Houston	Houston	USA	5,800,000	
64	Miami	Miami *incl. Ft. Lauderdale, W. Palm Beach*	USA	5,750,000	

65	Bandung	Bandung	Indonesia	5,600,000
65	Detroit	Detroit *incl. Toledo, Windsor (Canada)*	USA	5,600,000
67	Nanjing	Nanking	China	5,400,000
67	Pune	Poona *incl. Pimpri-Chinchwad*	India	5,400,000
69	Atlanta	Atlanta	USA	5,350,000
70	Al-Kharṭūm	Khartoum	Sudan	5,100,000
70	Sankt-Peterburg	Saint Petersburg	Russia	5,100,000
72	Milano	Milan	Italy	5,050,000
73	Sūrat	Surat	India	5,000,000
73	Yangon	Rangoon	Myanmar	5,000,000
75	Chittagong	Chittagong	Bangladesh	4,875,000
76	Guadalajara	Guadalajara *incl. Zapopan*	Mexico	4,850,000
77	Al-Iskandarīyah	Alexandria	Egypt	4,775,000
78	Sydney	Sydney	Australia	4,700,000
79	Abidjan	Abidjan	Côte d'Ivoire	4,675,000
80	Shantou	Shantou	China	4,650,000
81	Ruhrgebiet	The Ruhr	Germany	4,625,000
82	Barcelona	Barcelona	Spain	4,600,000
82	Harbin	Harbin	China	4,600,000
82	Nairobi	Nairobi	Kenya	4,600,000
85	Caracas	Caracas	Venezuela	4,525,000
86	Monterrey	Monterrey	Mexico	4,500,000
87	Surabaya	Surabaya	Indonesia	4,450,000
88	Ankara	Ankara	Turkey	4,400,000
89	Berlin	Berlin	Germany	4,375,000
89	Hangzhou	Hangchou	China	4,375,000
91	Melbourne	Melbourne	Australia	4,225,000
92	Phoenix	Phoenix	USA	4,175,000
92	Porto Alegre	Porto Alegre	Brazil	4,175,000
94	Accra	Accra	Ghana	4,150,000
95	Napoli	Naples	Italy	4,125,000
96	Casablanca	Casablanca	Morocco	4,100,000
97	Brasília	Brasília	Brazil	4,075,000
97	Cape Town	Cape Town	South Africa	4,075,000
99	Qingdao	Tsingtao	China	4,000,000
100	Montréal	Montreal	Canada	3,975,000
100	Recife	Recife	Brazil	3,975,000

102	Tampa	Tampa incl. Lakeland, St. Petersburg, Sarasota	USA	3,900,000
103	Seattle	Seattle	USA	3,875,000
104	Fortaleza	Fortaleza	Brazil	3,850,000
105	Al-Kuwayt	Kuwait City	Kuwait	3,825,000
105	Durban	Durban	South Africa	3,825,000
107	Jiddah	Jidda	Saudi Arabia	3,800,000
108	Kano	Kano	Nigeria	3,775,000
109	Salvador	Salvador	Brazil	3,750,000
110	Medellín	Medellín	Colombia	3,700,000
111	Taiyuan	Taiyuan	China	3,675,000
112	Dalian	Dairen	China	3,650,000
113	Busan	Pusan	S. Korea	3,625,000
114	Faisalabad	Faisalabad	Pakistan	3,600,000
115	Changchun	Changchun	China	3,550,000
115	Jinan	Jinan	China	3,550,000
117	Zhengzhou	Zhengzhou	China	3,525,000
118	Dar es Salaam	Dar es Salaam	Tanzania	3,500,000
119	Athínai	Athens	Greece	3,475,000
119	Rāwalpindi	Rawalpindi incl. Islamabad	Pakistan	3,475,000
121	Dimashq	Damascus	Syria	3,425,000
121	Kānpur	Kanpur	India	3,425,000
123	Curitiba	Curitiba	Brazil	3,400,000
123	Roma	Rome	Italy	3,400,000
125	Santo Domingo	Santo Domingo	Dominican Republic	3,375,000
126	El Djazaïr	Algiers	Algeria	3,350,000
127	Jaipur	Jaipur	India	3,300,000
128	Denver	Denver	USA	3,275,000
128	Kābol	Kabul	Afghanistan	3,275,000
130	Kyïv	Kiev	Ukraine	3,250,000
130	Lucknow	Lucknow	India	3,250,000
130	Medan	Medan	Indonesia	3,250,000
133	Kunming	Kunming	China	3,225,000
134	Adis Abeba	Addis Abeba	Ethiopia	3,200,000
135	'Ammān	Amman	Jordan	3,150,000
135	Fuzhou	Fuzhou	China	3,150,000
137	San Diego	San Diego	USA	3,125,000

138	Cleveland	Cleveland *incl. Akron*	USA	3,075,000
139	Campinas	Campinas	Brazil	3,050,000
139	Harare	Harare	Zimbabwe	3,050,000
141	Minneapolis	Minneapolis	USA	2,950,000
142	Puebla	Puebla	Mexico	2,925,000
143	Changsha	Changsha	China	2,900,000
143	Orlando	Orlando	USA	2,900,000
145	İzmir	Izmir	Turkey	2,875,000
146	Cali	Cali	Colombia	2,850,000
146	Mashhad	Meshed	Iran	2,850,000
146	Rotterdam	Rotterdam *incl.- Gravenhage* (*The Hague*)	Netherlands	2,850,000
149	Dakar	Dakar	Senegal	2,825,000
149	Ḥalab	Aleppo	Syria	2,825,000
151	Ciudad de Guatemala	Guatemala City	Guatemala	2,800,000
151	Ibadan	Ibadan	Nigeria	2,800,000
153	Gaoxiong	Kaohsiung	Taiwan (Rep. of China)	2,775,000
153	Nāgpur	Nagpur	India	2,775,000
155	P'yŏngyang	Pyongyang	N. Korea	2,725,000
156	Cincinnati	Cincinnati *incl. Dayton*	USA	2,700,000
156	Hà Nội	Hanoi	Vietnam	2,700,000
156	Pretoria	Pretoria	S. Africa	2,700,000
156	Wenzhou	Wenzhou	China	2,700,000
160	Birmingham	Birmingham	G. Britain	2,675,000
160	Shijiazhuang	Shijiazhuang	China	2,675,000
162	Hamburg	Hamburg	Germany	2,650,000
162	Manchester	Manchester	G.Britain	2,650,000
164	Daegu	Taegu	S. Korea	2,625,000
164	Guayaquil	Guayaquil	Ecuador	2,625,000
164	Urumqi	Urumqi	China	2,625,000
167	Port-au-Prince	Port-au-Prince	Haiti	2,600,000
168	Lisboa	Lisbon	Portugal	2,575,000
169	Budapest	Budapest	Hungary	2,550,000
169	Hefei	Hofei	China	2,550,000
169	Toshkent	Tashkent	Uzbekistan	2,550,000
172	Bamako	Bamako	Mali	2,525,000
172	Douala	Douala	Cameroon	2,525,000

172	Guiyang	Guiyang	China	2,525,000
172	Sapporo	Sapporo	Japan	2,525,000
172	Wuxi	Wuxi	China	2,525,000
172	Zibo	Zibo	China	2,525,000
178	Fukuoka	Fukuoka	Japan	2,475,000
178	Xiamen	Xiamen	China	2,475,000
180	Colombo	Colombo	Sri Lanka	2,450,000
180	Katowice	Katowice *including Upper Silesian Area*	Poland	2,450,000
182	Lanzhou	Lanzhou	China	2,425,000
182	Tūnis	Tunis	Tunisia	2,425,000
182	Vancouver	Vancouver	Canada	2,425,000
182	Yaoundé	Yaoundé	Cameroon	2,425,000
186	Tel Aviv-Yafo	Tel Aviv-Jaffa	Israel	2,375,000
187	Bakı	Baku	Azerbaijan	2,350,000
187	Indore	Indore	India	2,350,000
187	St. Louis	St. Louis	USA	2,350,000
190	Asunción	Asunción	Paraguay	2,325,000
190	Bhilai	Bhilai *including Raipur*	India	2,325,000
190	Coimbatore	Coimbatore	India	2,325,000
190	Kāṭhmāḍaŭ	Kathmandu	Nepal	2,325,000
190	Kumasi	Kumasi	Ghana	2,325,000
190	Patna	Patna	India	2,325,000
196	Nanchang	Nanchang	China	2,300,000
196	Ningbo	Ningbo	China	2,300,000
196	Taizhong	Taichung	Taiwan (R. of China)	2,300,000
199	Leeds	Leeds	G. Britain	2,275,000
199	San Juan	San Juan	Puerto Rico	2,275,000
201	Warszawa	Warsaw	Poland	2,250,000
202	Anshan	Anshan *including Liaoyang*	China	2,225,000
202	Belém	Belém	Brazil	2,225,000
202	Gujrānwāla	Gujranwala	Pakistan	2,225,000
202	La Habana	Havana	Cuba	2,225,000
202	Ṣanʻāʼ	Sana'a	Yemen	2,225,000
207	Antananarivo	Tananarive	Madagascar	2,200,000
207	Charlotte	Charlotte	USA	2,200,000
207	Goiânia	Goiânia	Brazil	2,200,000
207	Hyderābād	Hyderabad	Pakistan	2,200,000
207	Portland	Portland	USA	2,200,000

207	Salt Lake City	Salt Lake City *incl. Ogden, Provo*	USA	2,200,000
213	Eşfahān	Isfahan	Iran	2,175,000
213	Kampala	Kampala	Uganda	2,175,000
215	Ad-Dammām	Dammam	Saudi Arabia	2,150,000
216	Brisbane	Brisbane	Australia	2,125,000
216	Nanning	Nanning	China	2,125,000
218	Stockholm	Stockholm	Sweden	2,100,000
219	Cebu	Cebu	Philippines	2,075,000
219	Las Vegas	Las Vegas	USA	2,075,000
219	München	Munich	Germany	2,075,000
219	Quanzhou	Quanzhou	China	2,075,000
223	Pittsburgh	Pittsburgh	USA	2,050,000
223	Tangshan	Tangshan	China	2,050,000
223	Wien	Vienna	Austria	2,050,000
226	La Paz	La Paz	Bolivia	2,025,000
226	Maputo	Maputo	Mozambique	2,025,000
228	Bhopāl	Bhopal	India	2,000,000
228	Toluca	Toluca	Mexico	2,000,000
230	Maracaibo	Maracaibo	Venezuela	1,990,000
230	Stuttgart	Stuttgart	Germany	1,990,000
232	Huizhou	Huizhou	China	1,980,000
232	Lusaka	Lusaka	Zambia	1,980,000
232	Multān	Multan	Pakistan	1,980,000
235	Amsterdam	Amsterdam *Incl. Haarlem*	Netherlamds	1,970,000
235	Rabat	Rabat	Morocco	1,970,000
237	Bruxelles	Brussels	Belgium	1,960,000
237	Semarang	Semarang	Indonesia	1,960,000
239	Changzhou	Changzhou	China	1,950,000
239	Frankfurt	Frankfurt	Germany	1,950,000
239	Sacramento	Sacramento	USA	1,950,000
242	Manaus	Manaus	Brazil	1,940,000
243	Barranquilla	Barranquilla	Colombia	1,920,000
243	San Antonio	San Antonio	USA	1,920,000
243	Vadodara	Vadodara	India	1,920,000
246	Köln	Cologne	Germany	1,910,000
247	Kansas City	Kansas City	USA	1,890,000
247	Tijuana	Tijuana	Mexico	1,890,000
249	Minsk	Minsk	Belarus	1,880,000
249	Ouagadou-gou	Ouagadougou	Burkina Faso	1,880,000
251	Āgra	Agra	India	1,870,000

251	Indianapolis	Indianapolis	USA	1,870,000
251	Santa Cruz	Santa Cruz	Bolivia	1,870,000
254	Hiroshima	Hiroshima	Japan	1,860,000
255	Visāk-hapatnam	Vishak-hapatnam	India	1,850,000
256	Jilin	Jilin	China	1,840,000
257	Baotou	Baotou	China	1,830,000
257	Bursa	Bursa	Turkey	1,830,000
257	Port Harcourt	Port Harcourt	Nigeria	1,830,000
260	Valencia	Valencia	Venezuela	1,820,000
261	San Salvador	San Salvador	El Salvador	1,810,000
261	Vitória	Vitória	Brazil	1,810,000
263	Santos	Santos	Brazil	1,800,000
264	Perth	Perth	Australia	1,790,000
265	Bucureşti	Bucharest	Romania	1,780,000
265	Montevideo	Montevideo	Uruguay	1,780,000
267	San José	San José	Costa Rica	1,770,000
268	Conakry	Conakry	Guinea	1,760,000
269	León	León	Mexico	1,750,000
270	Peshāwar	Peshawar	Pakistan	1,730,000
270	Quito	Quito	Ecuador	1,730,000
272	Dubayy	Dubai	United Arab Emirates	1,720,000
272	Valencia	Valencia	Spain	1,720,000
274	Hartford	Hartford *incl. Springfield, MA*	USA	1,710,000
274	Ludhiāna	Ludhiana	India	1,710,000
274	Nižnij Novgorod	Nizhny Novgorod	Russia	1,710,000
277	Brazzaville	Brazzaville	Congo (Rep.)	1,700,000
277	Makkah	Mecca	Saudi Arabia	1,700,000
277	Meerut	Meerut	India	1,700,000
280	Lubumbashi	Lubumbashi	Congo (D. Rep.)	1,690,000
281	Nāshik	Nasik	India	1,680,000
281	Torino	Turin	Italy	1,680,000
283	Ad-Dawḥah	Doha	Qatar	1,660,000
283	Kochi	Cochin	India	1,660,000
283	Mbuji-Mayi	Mbuji-Mayi	Congo (D. Rep.)	1,660,000
286	Makassar	Makassar	Indonesia	1,650,000
287	Almaty	Alma-Ata	Kazakhstan	1,640,000
288	Kaduna	Kaduna	Nigeria	1,630,000
289	Adana	Adana	Turkey	1,620,000

290	Phnum Pénh	Phnom Penh	Cambodia	1,610,000
290	Vijayawāda	Vijayawada	India	1,610,000
292	Columbus	Columbus	USA	1,600,000
292	Palembang	Palembang	Indonesia	1,600,000
294	Austin	Austin	USA	1,590,000
294	Chandīgarh	Chandigarh	India	1,590,000
294	Charkiv	Kharkov	Ukraine	1,590,000
294	Ghazzah	Gaza	Palestinian Territories	1,590,000
294	Muqdisho	Mogadishu	Somalia	1,590,000
299	Marseille	Marseille	France	1,580,000
299	Virginia Beach	Virginia Beach incl. Norfolk	USA	1,580,000
301	Huainan	Huainan	China	1,570,000
301	Kitakyūshū	Kitakyushu	Japan	1,570,000
301	Lyon	Lyon	France	1,570,000
301	Qiqihar	Qiqihar	China	1,570,000
301	Sendai	Sendai	Japan	1,570,000
306	Gwangju	Kwangju	S. Korea	1,560,000
306	Tabrīz	Tabriz	Iran	1,560,000
306	Weifang	Weifang	China	1,560,000
306	Xuzhou	Xuzhou	China	1,560,000
306	Yantai	Yantai	China	1,560,000
311	Lomé	Lomé	Togo	1,550,000
311	Madurai	Madurai	India	1,550,000
313	Novosibirsk	Novosibirsk	Russia	1,540,000
314	Abuja	Abuja	Nigeria	1,530,000
314	Al-Mawşil	Mosul	Iraq	1,530,000
314	Daejeon	Taejon	S. Korea	1,530,000
314	Milwaukee	Milwaukee	USA	1,530,000
318	Khulna	Khulna	Bangladesh	1,520,000
318	Luoyang	Luoyang	China	1,520,000
318	Vārānasi	Benares	India	1,520,000
321	Jekaterinburg	Yekaterinburg	Russia	1,510,000
322	Córdoba	Córdoba	Argentina	1,500,000
322	Rājkot	Rajkot	India	1,500,000
324	Xiangfan	Xiangfan	China	1,490,000
324	Zhuhai	Zhuhai	China	1,490,000
326	Bhubaneswar	Bhubaneswar incl. Cuttack	India	1,480,000
326	Ciudad Juárez	Ciudad Juárez	Mexico	1,480,000
328	Liuzhou	Liuzhou	China	1,470,000

329	København	Copen-hagen	Denmark	1,460,000
329	Yangzhou	Yangzhou	China	1,460,000
331	Haikou	Haikou	China	1,450,000
332	Asansol	Asansol	India	1,440,000
332	Donėc'k	Donetsk	Ukraine	1,440,000
334	Benin City	Benin City	Nigeria	1,430,000
334	George Town	George Town	Malaysia	1,430,000
334	Glasgow	Glasgow	G. Britain	1,430,000
334	Okayama	Okayama	Japan	1,430,000
338	Jamshedpur	Jamshedpur	India	1,420,000
338	Praha	Prague	Czech Rep.	1,420,000
338	Raleigh	Raleigh	USA	1,420,000
338	Volgograd	Volgograd	Russia	1,420,000
342	Taizhou	Taizhou	China	1,410,000
343	Auckland	Auckland	New Zealand	1,400,000
343	Gaziantep	Gaziantep	Turkey	1,400,000
343	São Luís	São Luís	Brazil	1,400,000
346	Linyi	Linyi	China	1,390,000
347	Cixi	Cixi	China	1,380,000
348	Beograd	Belgrade	Serbia	1,370,000
348	Niamey	Niamey	Niger	1,370,000
348	Shīrāz	Shiraz	Iran	1,370,000
351	Malang	Malang	Indonesia	1,360,000
351	Sevilla	Sevilla	Spain	1,360,000
351	Srīnagar	Srinagar	India	1,360,000
354	Daqing	Daqing	China	1,350,000
354	Dnipro-pėtrovs'k	Dnepro-petrovsk	Ukraine	1,350,000
354	Liverpool	Liverpool	G. Britain	1,350,000
357	Hohhot	Huhehot	China	1,340,000
357	Jabalpur	Jabalpur	India	1,340,000
357	Natal	Natal	Brazil	1,340,000
360	Al-Manāmah	Manama	Bahrain	1,330,000
360	Čel'abinsk	Chelyabinsk	Russia	1,330,000
360	Sheffield	Sheffield	G. Britain	1,330,000
363	Buffalo	Buffalo *incl. St. Catharines (Canada)*	USA	1,320,000
364	Bayrūt	Beirut	Lebanon	1,310,000
364	Ciudad de Panamá	Panama City	Panama	1,310,000
364	Denpasar	Denpasar	Indonesia	1,310,000
364	Samara	Samara	Russia	1,310,000
364	Sofija	Sofia	Bulgaria	1,310,000

369	Datong	Datong	China	1,300,000
369	Freetown	Freetown	Sierra Leone	1,300,000
369	Torreón	Torreón	Mexico	1,300,000
372	Allahābād	Allahabad	India	1,290,000
372	Harrisburg	Harrisburg *incl. Lancaster, York*	USA	1,290,000
372	Jacksonville	Jacksonville	USA	1,290,000
372	Nashville	Nashville	USA	1,290,000
372	Ottawa	Ottawa	Canada	1,290,000
372	Rosario	Rosario	Argentina	1,290,000
378	Aurangābād	Aurangabad	India	1,280,000
378	Calgary	Calgary	Canada	1,280,000
378	Dublin	Dublin	Ireland	1,280,000
378	Tainan	Tainan	Taiwan(R. of China)	1,280,000
382	Dhanbād	Dhanbad	India	1,270,000
383	Mannheim	Mannheim	Germany	1,260,000
383	Maracay	Maracay	Venezuela	1,260,000
383	Ṭarābulus	Tripoli	Libya	1,260,000
383	Tbilisi	Tbilisi	Georgia	1,260,000
387	Al-Baṣrah	Basra	Iraq	1,250,000
387	Amritsar	Amritsar	India	1,250,000
387	Ash-Shāriqah	Sharjah	United Arab Emirates	1,250,000
387	Managua	Managua	Nicaragua	1,250,000
387	Rostov-na-Donu	Rostov-on-Don	Russia	1,250,000
392	Davao	Davao	Philippines	1,240,000
392	Lille	Lille *incl. Kortrijk (Belgium)*	France	1,240,000
392	Maceió	Maceió	Brazil	1,240,000
392	Yerevan	Yerevan	Armenia	1,240,000
396	Adelaide	Adelaide	Australia	1,230,000
396	Cartagena	Cartagena	Colombia	1,230,000
396	Düsseldorf	Dusseldorf	Germany	1,230,000
396	McAllen	McAllen *incl. Brownsville*	USA	1,230,000
396	Yogyakarta	Yogyakarta	Indonesia	1,230,000
401	Barquisi-meto	Barquisi-meto	Venezuela	1,220,000
401	Cotonou	Cotonou	Benin	1,220,000
401	Edmonton	Edmonton	Canada	1,220,000
401	Jodhpur	Jodhpur	India	1,220,000
405	Al-Madīnah	Medina	Saudi Arabia	1,210,000

405	Monrovia	Monrovia	Liberia	1,210,000
405	Zürich	Zurich	Switzerland	1,210,000
408	Querétaro	Querétaro	Mexico	1,200,000
408	Rānchi	Ranchi	India	1,200,000
410	Joinville	Joinville	Brazil	1,190,000
411	Mudanjiang	Mudanjiang	China	1,180,000
411	Oran	Oran	Algeria	1,180,000
411	Porto	Porto	Portugal	1,180,000
411	Stockton	Stockton *incl. Modesto*	USA	1,180,000
415	Cochabamba	Cochabamba	Bolivia	1,170,000
415	Gwalior	Gwalior	India	1,170,000
415	Surakarta	Surakarta	Indonesia	1,170,000
415	Yiwu	Yiwu	China	1,170,000
419	Fès	Fes	Morocco	1,160,000
419	Ulaanbaatar	Ulan Bator	Mongolia	1,160,000
421	Kazan'	Kazan	Russia	1,150,000
421	Memphis	Memphis	USA	1,150,000
421	Naha	Naha	Japan	1,150,000
421	Ndjamena	Ndjamena	Chad	1,150,000
421	Omsk	Omsk	Russia	1,150,000
421	Ulsan	Ulsan	S. Korea	1,150,000
427	Helsinki	Helsinki	Finland	1,140,000
427	João Pessoa	João Pessoa	Brazil	1,140,000
429	Ahvāz	Ahvaz	Iran	1,130,000
429	Himeji	Himeji	Japan	1,130,000
429	Valparaíso	Valparaíso	Chile	1,130,000
432	Newcastle upon Tyne	Newcastle upon Tyne	G. Britain	1,120,000
432	Zhanjiang	Zhanjiang	China	1,120,000
434	Baoding	Baoding	China	1,110,000
434	Bucara-manga	Bucara-manga	Colombia	1,110,000
434	Hamamatsu	Hamamatsu	Japan	1,110,000
434	Kumamoto	Kumamoto	Japan	1,110,000
434	Melbourne	Melbourne *incl. Palm Bay, Port St. Lucie*	USA	1,110,000
434	San Luis Potosí	San Luis Potosí	Mexico	1,110,000
434	Thiruvanantha-apuram	Trivandrum	India	1,110,000
441	Bulawayo	Bulawayo	Zimbabwe	1,100,000
441	Maiduguri	Maiduguri	Nigeria	1,100,000

441	Qom	Qom	Iran	1,100,000
441	Tai'an	Tai'an	China	1,100,000
441	Xining	Xining	China	1,100,000
446	Konya	Konya	Turkey	1,090,000
446	Mandalay	Mandalay	Myanmar	1,090,000
446	Port Elizabeth	Port Elizabeth	South Africa	1,090,000
449	Changwon	Changwon	S. Korea	1,080,000
449	Florianópolis	Florianópolis	Brazil	1,080,000
449	Greensboro	Greensboro	USA	1,080,000
449	Kota	Kota	India	1,080,000
449	Tiruchirāppalli	Tiruchirappalli	India	1,080,000
454	Odésa	Odessa	Ukraine	1,070,000
454	Saratov	Saratov	Russia	1,070,000
454	Ufa	Ufa	Russia	1,070,000
454	Zaozhuang	Zaozhuang	China	1,070,000
458	Arbīl	Erbil	Iraq	1,060,000
458	Aşgabat	Ashgabat	Turkmenistan	1,060,000
458	Nürnberg	Nuremberg	Germany	1,060,000
458	Quetta	Quetta	Pakistan	1,060,000
458	Tegucigalpa	Tegucigalpa	Honduras	1,060,000
463	Bareilly	Bareilly	India	1,050,000
463	Shaoxing	Shaoxing	China	1,050,000
463	Tiruppūr	Tirupur	India	1,050,000
466	Jining	Jining	China	1,040,000
466	Kozhikode	Calicut	India	1,040,000
466	Mérida	Mérida	Mexico	1,040,000
466	Mysore	Mysore	India	1,040,000
466	Oklahoma City	Oklahoma City	USA	1,040,000
466	Pekanbaru	Pekanbaru	Indonesia	1,040,000
466	Perm'	Perm	Russia	1,040,000
466	Yueyang	Yueyang	China	1,040,000
474	Antalya	Antalya	Turkey	1,030,000
474	Guilin	Guilin	China	1,030,000
474	Guwāhāti	Gauhati	India	1,030,000
474	Zhuzhou	Zhuzhou	China	1,030,000
478	Bandar Lampung	Bandar Lampung	Indonesia	1,020,000
478	Batam	Batam	Indonesia	1,020,000
478	Jixi	Jixi	China	1,020,000
478	Louisville	Louisville	USA	1,020,000
478	Mombasa	Mombasa	Kenya	1,020,000
478	Nouakchott	Nouakchott	Mauritania	1,020,000
478	Pingdingshan	Pingdingshan	China	1,020,000

485	Aguascalientes	Aguascalientes	Mexico	1,010,000
485	El Paso	El Paso *incl. Las Cruces*	USA	1,010,000
485	Kirkūk	Kirkuk	Iraq	1,010,000
485	Krasnojarsk	Krasnoyarsk	Russia	1,010,000
485	Marrakech	Marrakech	Morocco	1,010,000
490	Angeles	Angeles	Philippines	1,000,000
490	Antwerpen	Antwerp	Belgium	1,000,000
490	Handan	Handan	China	1,000,000
490	Hubli-Dhārwār	Hubli-Dharwar	India	1,000,000
490	Mexicali	Mexicali	Mexico	1,000,000
490	Richmond	Richmond	USA	1,000,000
490	Serang	Serang	Indonesia	1,000,000
490	Solāpur	Sholapur	India	1,000,000
490	Yichang	Yichang	China	1,000,000

INDEX